# Welcome To Hell

by

Elizabeth Simpson

ISBN: 978-1-935802-35-8

**FATHER
&
SON**
PUBLISHING, INC.
4909 N. Monroe Street
Tallahassee, Florida 32303-7015
www.fatherson.com
800-741-2712

# Dedication

I dedicate this book to my Lord and Savior, Jesus, as He is the one who inspired me to write this book. My hope is that this book will cause Christian readers to see the urgency to lead many souls to God's saving grace so they can avoid an eternity in Hell as described in this book. If you are not a Christian, please turn to God and receive His salvation through Jesus Christ, the only way to salvation.

# Introduction

Dear Reader,

Proceed reading this book carefully. It is rather descriptive and, in part, disturbing and not for just anyone to read. However, if you choose to read it, then I request that you read it in its entirety and not stop half way through, as challenging as it may be.

The subject matter of this story will upset many. In fact, I don't pretend that this book will not be shunned in some circles. The subject of Hell is rarely spoken of and it seems even less spoken of in church. Society likes to pretend that Hell does not exist, and when they hint that it might, they make light of it.

Reader, in your own walk of life, have you experienced moments where you felt as though you were "walking through hell" or something very near it? Many of us have. Even I have felt as though what I was going through could not be much better than Hell itself. Believe me when I say that the worst thing you could imagine someone going through, even if it is something you went through yourself, does not scrape the surface of what Hell is truly like.

So why did I write this book? God placed this story on my heart to write and I obeyed. It has taken me nearly a decade and a half to complete this book, mainly due to the subject matter. This is a dark novel, not happy in the least. There were many and quite long pauses in the writing of this, but near the end of its completion, I found it much easier to focus on the writing, as though this book was meant for now.

This story is a warning, not meant to be taken lightly. So reader, when you are finished with this book, you will have a choice. I hope you choose well.

# Contents

Elizabeth Simpson was born and raised in Florida, where she resides today with her husband and child. Since birth, God's word has been poured into her and all her church life has been in a Pentecostal/Charismatic church. She tells people she spoke in tongues before she learned to speak English.

In elementary school, Elizabeth was diagnosed with dyslexia and even was told by one of her teachers that she would never make it as a writer. What her teacher didn't realize is that when Elizabeth is told that something is impossible, or very hard to do, she is determined to prove she can do it. One of her earliest memory verses was Philippians 4:13, "I can do all things through Christ who strengthens me."

Today, Elizabeth is still attending the same church ministry that she grew up in. She has been a member of the worship team, served as worship leader, taught Sunday School, hosted and led a prayer group, helped with the church's food pantry, organized church events, and has helped the church ministry in many other ways, even serving as church janitor.

Elizabeth also loves to write Christian drama and has presented many plays at her church. She loves to write and plans to continue writing as long as God pours the ideas into her.

# 1

## Where? How? Why?

The first thing one observes when they find themselves in a place that is unknown to them is what they see around them that is known to them. When one cannot fathom as to how or why they have arrived in a strange place, they desperately search out something that is not quite as strange. They try to learn what they can by what they see. They look for something that is familiar, whether it is as common as a Taco Bell or as trivial as a bus stop, anything that will assure them that though this is not home, it isn't the end of the universe. As for me, it had to be the end of the universe.

What does the end of the universe look like? Absolutely nothing. There is nothing. Not a star, not a single flicker of light, not even a fleck. I see nothing. Not a cloud, not a single color. I cannot even call this black. I have seen black, and this is not it.

My eyes are open, or are they? I cannot tell. I felt for my eyes, but I failed to make contact with my face. I do have hands don't I? I could have sworn I opened my eyes. And yet, nothing, nothing but an abyss remained around me, my vision void of any defining thing, not even light—the absence of light—extreme darkness. Even the blind would confess that they see even less here.

If there is something that is blacker than black, I was looking at it. Perhaps my eyes were closed after all and this abyss is a nightmare. Perhaps none of this is real. Again, I decided that I must have been asleep having a horrible dream. I opened my eyes, or were they already open? How long had my eyes been closed? I blinked, at least, I think I blinked. I blinked again. I could not tell whether I was blinking or not. I could not feel the motion of blinking. I can blink, right? I thought I knew how to, I thought I had blinked before, but now I'm not so sure.

Either way, I still could see nothing, less than nothing. How long had I been wherever I am? And exactly where was I? I could not see, but I distinctly remember that I had no impairment in my vision, at least, before that moment, I had not been blind, so maybe, just maybe it was as simple as the lights being off in a windowless room. I can't be blind. I don't remember going blind. I don't remember anything that would have caused me to go blind, so the lights must be off.

I soon came to the realization that I could hear nothing either. Even in silence, there is noise—buzzing, humming, a heartbeat, but in that particular moment in time there was nothing. I could not even hear my own breathing. I was breathing, wasn't I? I was afraid to speak, afraid to confirm what I already suspected to be true.

Slowly, I ordered my thoughts to open my mouth and try to say 'hello.' I heard nothing, and though I was not convinced that I had actually succeeded in saying anything, I was too afraid to try again.

So I was blind and deaf! A sudden rush of doom encompassed me and imprinted itself on my soul. From that point on, doom remained with me, or was it later that doom made itself known to me?

I checked my olfactory sense and found that I could not smell.

Without being able to eat anything or drink anything, I could not test my taste, however I could not distinguish the taste of the air or even my own saliva.

Suddenly I was seized with terror as I came to the realization that I could not feel anything. I could not feel the rise and fall of my chest. I could not feel any sensation of my body, neither pain nor numbness, as though I no longer had a body. It was as though the only thing left of me was thought. Oh, if only this had been the case.

My mind worked—I was conscious, and yet, I could not command my body to do a thing. I cannot tell you if I moved. I cannot tell you if I did anything, except wonder, wonder how I came to be in my present situation and what my present situation was. Perhaps I was in a coma, forced to live inside myself. If only I could have remained in that unknown moment. If I had known, I would have chosen that, I think.

If I was in a coma, then perhaps I could wake myself. Perhaps being aware that there was life outside of this … actual real living … was all I needed to wake myself. The yearning, the desire to not be comatose should snap me out of it, right? Perhaps. If. Those two words plagued me.

I felt awake.

And just as quickly as the terror had seized me, a sensation like no other encompassed my body. A pain of great magnitude, as though all of my atoms had been separated and were now coming back together, stung every pore of my being. The pain faded quickly, but I sensed that that pain was just a taste of what was to come.

I tried to feel for my eyes again. This time I could feel my face. I decided that the touch was a sure indicator that I was now definitely awake.

I wanted to be awake. I wanted to see again. With what hope I could muster, I yelled, "Why can't I see?!" Possibly someone would hear me. Possibly they would let me know what is wrong with me. This time I did hear my voice. I heard every word clearly. Maybe I was coming out of the coma.

That first yell opened up all my senses and I began to take note first of what I could hear and see. I took the chance again and yelled into my darkness, "Can anyone turn on the lights?" Just maybe this was all a mistake, all a joke and I really wasn't blind or in a coma. Waiting for a reply, I only received a disappointing silence, though at least now I could hear a steady faint high-pitched whine.

I didn't want to be blind. I wanted to see. I wanted to make out my surroundings visually. I wanted to see, and since I could not remember a reason as to why I could not, I decided that since I could hear then I might still be able to see. It had to be as simple as the lights being off. The lights had to be off. I couldn't accept any other explanation.

"Lights!" I screamed. "Lights please!" I demanded. "Is there anyone there?" I begged.

In the seemingly near distance, yet coming from no particular direction, a strange gurgling groan erupted. Too stunned to be afraid and not knowing what I should think or feel, I gave it one last shot to communicate with the darkness and now the unpleasant sound.

"I can hear you. I know you're there. Speak up." More groaning was the only reply. "Are you okay?" I asked, though I really didn't care. I had my own problems.

4

No one turned on any lights. Either there was no one around, which I was beginning to feel quite alone, or I was blind and no one had the courage to tell me. I accepted this with dread and great hesitation—to be blind—it was better than the alternatives I had already wondered about and much better than the fact that I was soon to learn.

How would I go about life blind? Blind people do it all the time. There would be an adjustment period for me. I didn't want to be blind, but what visually impaired person wants to be blind? And why isn't there someone here to help me?! I turned around looking for someone. What a joke! Looking! I couldn't see a thing!

I was standing, though I don't remember getting up. Then again, I don't remember ever laying down or sitting down. I don't know what I could remember. I took a step forward then remembered I couldn't see. I used my feet to navigate. While balancing on one leg, I dragged the other foot along the ground. My arms hung in the air for balance. I didn't wish to fall, though not so much wishing. I had this fear that something dreadful would come from me hitting the floor.

Using my senses of touch and hearing, I deduced that I was standing on loose gravel, maybe even a sandy path, though I didn't feel as though I was outside. There was no wind, nor warmth from the sun. Nothing chirped, croaked, or scurried. The only noises that could be heard were pebbles and dirt scraping against the bottom of my shoe and the groan that now erupted periodically.

I wasn't one to venture out at night, not alone at least. At least, I knew that much about myself, but that didn't answer any questions. I still couldn't see, nor did I know where on earth I managed to place myself. Inch by inch, I made a full circle, or at least, what seemed to be a circle of my very near surroundings. There was nothing. I didn't want to stay there in the dark, alone. I wanted to see, at that point I didn't really care what I would see, just that I could see would suffice.

If I had known then, what I know now, I would have never wished to see again. In fact, I would have wished to be deaf, too.

Slowly, my eyes began to adjust to the blackness, or maybe it was the simple fact that someone turned on a light somewhere. Either way, I could finally make out my surroundings, though dim as it remained. I could see! I'm not blind! And yet, shock and horror enveloped me immediately. I turned from one jutting rock face to another. I didn't know what to think. I couldn't fathom a clue as to why I would be standing in a cave. Not really a cave either, though I was surrounded by rock on all sides. For Heaven's sake I'm claustrophobic! I shrunk back in fear. I was never claustrophobic before, but in that instant I was claustrophobic. I owned claustrophobia. I became claustrophobia. What on earth possessed me to enter such a place? What would cause me to take on one of my strongest fears, a fear I never knew before that moment?

I wrung my hands through my hair. I can't remember! Why can't I remember? "Let me out of here!" I screamed. Though I knew no one would. I wasn't even convinced that there was anyone there that could hear me. I was there alone with the walls that closed in around me, groans that didn't belong to anything but the walls. But there had to be someone else there, otherwise, what made the noise? My imagination? My desperation to not be trapped alone? I beat my fist against my forehead; I had to remember. This all had to be a nightmare.

I couldn't explain what made me feel so desperate. I tended to be calm and collected in all situations. Then again, I also tended to not get trapped inside small places with no way out. I felt as if someone had taken out the rational section of my brain. I couldn't make sense of anything! Terror invaded my thoughts and feelings, poking and teasing me into a state of irrationality—a state of insanity. I could not focus on any one thing. My mind raced from being trapped, to being alone, to trying to remember, to where I was, to the walls closing in on me, to the groaning, and then back again to being trapped; the cycle repeating itself until my heart raced as fast as my thoughts and my head pounded as though something in my brain was trying to get out through my temples.

Needing answers, I began with the most important and basic question: who am I? I paused as I searched my thoughts. Who am I? Oh God, I can't remember. Calm yourself. Close your eyes and picture yourself in more pleasant surroundings. I rubbed my temples with my fingertips. I couldn't picture pleasant surroundings, but at least, I could close my eyes. 'I'm not surrounded by rocks. I'm not surrounded by rocks,' I repeated in my mind over and over. I wrapped my arms around myself and swayed. I didn't want to sit. I didn't want to feel the dirt and rocks beneath me. I didn't want this reality to be true.

Now I have amnesia. I could not remember one thing from my past. Did I have a past? Did I understand what a past was? Either way, I could not remember. What is happening to me? What is wrong with me? Am I still in the coma? Was I ever in a coma? What is real? I opened my eyes and still all that surrounded me was hell. "Wake up!" I shouted at myself. "You idiot, wake up!" I shouted again. Why would anyone with any sense allow for this nightmare to continue?

I closed my eyes tight. Wake up, I ordered myself silently. I did not want to even hear my own voice now. I did not recognize it, though it had to be my voice. Didn't it? This wasn't some horrible sci-fi movie coming to reality? I didn't know what to think, or what to believe, or what was real. I just didn't want what was there, surrounding me, encompassing me in fear.

# 2

# What Now?

I opened my eyes and I was standing on a beautiful beach. The ocean was clear, a nice shade of aqua green. The sky was perfect, blue without a single cloud. The air was warm, not hot. I didn't want to close my eyes. It might disappear and I could not bare that.

How did I get here? Perhaps I had been asleep after all and the nightmare was finally over. Though, I still could not remember how I got to a beach. There was no one else in sight and for the moment, I did not care. I was not in that horrible place—that place which caused my darkest emotions and thoughts to recreate my being down to its cellular properties into something that I didn't want to be me.

I had become fear, not merely experiencing it, but fear flowed in my veins and had become part of my genetic makeup. I doubt if I am even making sense. You would have to experience it for yourself, though I hope you never do.

The beach at first glance was wonderful. At first glance, one doesn't always see the full picture. The hot sun seemed to keep getting hotter. The glare from the water hurt my eyes. The white sand on the beach also reflected the brightness of the sun and the burning warmth of its rays.

My skin soon felt as though it was on fire, and when I looked down at my arms, they were red with burn. I could see the blisters which covered every visible surface. My feet also hurt and when I directed my focus onto them, I saw a blood pool around them. The ground beneath me was not sand. There was broken glass everywhere. My feet were bare, and I was standing directly on the glass.

I screamed in pain and shock. I could not move. Every shift, every breath, caused my feet to slide further into the glass, cutting them all the way to the bones. One of my toes was mostly severed. Was this worse than the cave? Here, I felt physical pain. In the cave, I felt the emotions of fear and abandonment, which were manifesting themselves into physical pain, but at least I could bear that pain. Couldn't I?

# 3

# Back?

I screamed again when my balance shifted and my foot slid and a piece of glass shredded my heel up to my ankle. I hunched forward, though I had not wanted to move yet again. I closed my eyes as the pain increased well past my bearable level. I knew that at any moment I would faint from the pain. I did not. When I opened my eyes, there was darkness.

I closed my eyes again, helping my eyes to readjust quicker. After a few seconds, I opened my eyes again and peered into the dark.

What is happening? How do I end this? Where was I? For a few minutes, had I really left this place? Had I really been on a hot beach of broken glass? My feet still hurt. However, when I looked down, I couldn't even see my feet. I did slowly lift one foot. I felt no increase of pain from the movement and I gently tapped the one foot I balanced on. I was wearing shoes. I could not explain what happened.

I slowly felt for my arms. I didn't feel blisters, but my arms were warm to the touch. It had been so real. Was it merely an hallucination or is this the hallucination? Where is real? Would I know real if I was there? Confusion … chaos and confusion. My mind was a sea of confusion. My mind was my enemy. It fought me. It fought logic. It fought what was real. The pain was real, too real.

At some point I remembered that I still could not remember. Who am I?

My mind replayed that three-worded question over and over. I thought on the question and struggled with the question so hard that I broke into a cold sweat. Still, I could not come up with an answer. Perhaps if I don't dwell on it, the answer will just come to me in its own time. I just wish it wouldn't take such a long time. I needed to know.

I almost felt that if I knew the answer to who I was then I would have the answers to the other questions that had been tormenting me. Everything rested on me just knowing my own name. Who am I?

# 4

# Pain and Revelation

Who am I? I kept questioning. I closed my eyes but I could see light penetrating my lids, so I opened them. The room was brightly lit. The walls were white and padded. The rocks and sand had completely vanished. There were no doors or windows, and yet, I did not feel the claustrophobia that I had felt in the darkness. I did not feel physical pain either for the first time since this nightmare began. I did, however, feel humiliation.

I could not understand why I felt such humiliation. It was so heavy, I felt as though I was literally wearing it. Dropping my head, my eyes were shocked to see my naked body, and worse, I was filthy. Dirt and blood and only God knows what other vile mess covered my arms, legs and torso. I smelled of excrement and vomit. I don't know how I came to be this unclean. I wanted to hide under something, shower, put on clothes, but there was nothing there to satisfy any of those needs.

When I looked back up, all around the top of the wall where it met the ceiling were eyes, thousands of eyes bordering the upper walls and all of them were looking at my exposed and deplorable body. I could not hide. I felt as though I was being judged. I had no one to defend me. I stood there unable to hide from the prosecuting eyes, unable to clean myself. I was dirty and I felt dirty and I felt that they knew I was dirty, not only on the outside, but also on the inside.

I crouched in shame, covering most of my body with my arms and legs. I sat there with my arms wrapped around my knees tightly holding them to my chest. Propping my forehead on my knees, hoping that by not looking at the eyes, they would somehow disappear.

"Julia Chasen," a condescending voice screeched.

I slowly looked up toward the eyes. Julia, that's right, Julia Chasen. I am Julia Chasen.

"You have been found guilty," the same voice continued.

Guilty of what? Why am I naked? Why am I dirty? It was as though my lips had been sewn closed, because all I could do was scream these words in my thoughts. Not one syllable made it out of my mouth.

I closed my eyes, acting like an ostrich with his head in the ground, pretending that since I did not see them, they could not see me.

# 5

# Darkness

My eyes remained closed for a long time. After I had been 'found guilty,' they did not say another word to me. I still felt the shame, the guilt, the uncleanness, but my other senses told me that I was no longer in the white room.

I opened my eyes and darkness flooded my vision again.

I took in a great sigh of relief. My question was answered. Okay. So, why can't I remember how I got here? What happened to the beach or the white padded room? I felt my body and found that I was wearing clothes. Do I really care about the beach or the room? My skin was burnt and blistered, and my feet were marred while on the beach. In the room, I was completely exposed and then judged guilty. Was the beach the dream? Was the room the dream? Is this place the dream? Am

I hopping from one reality to another or is everything a dream? Am I the dream?

Was I going mad or am I already completely crazy? I was beginning to doubt my own existence.

I needed to get out of there. My fear kept me from focusing, and it most certainly kept me from remaining calm. My eyes had finally adjusted to the darkness again. Upon scanning the room again, something of which I had done several times over, my sight fell on what appeared to be a tunnel, and as I approached, it I could clearly make out stairs. My eyes fell to the scratches of fingernails and the marks of rudimentary tools such as rocks and sticks dug into each step, as though man's hands had made the stairway tunnel many centuries ago.

Was this a way out or was it only deception? To my dissatisfaction, the stairs spiraled downward into an unknown which led me to believe that this could merely be a ploy to draw me deeper into the earth. Perhaps there was another way out of that rocky chamber besides using the spiraling tunnel, one that I just could not see because someone had moved a bolder over the cave's mouth. Would it even help if I knew there was a way out, if I had found the huge rock blocking the way out? It wasn't like I could move it. Even if I was a man, chances are I could not budge it. I glanced around and could not detect that there were any other openings, blocked or otherwise, in the cave. My only way out of that room was to take the stairs.

I had no desire to head even deeper into … well … into whatever or wherever it would take me. I wanted to follow the light, but the orangey glow seemed to come from no apparent light source. The dimness was constant around me, no shadows, no brighter spots, nor dimmer. With my only other alternative being to stay where I was at, I chose to risk the stairs and placed a foot on the top step. I mustered up what hope I could conjure and placed all of it in finding a way out. If only I had remained in that room. Could have I remained or would there still have been the draw, pulling me to take the stairs? We shall never know. Then again, I had been most desperate to find a way out, and that in itself was a draw.

The stairs from the cave had been the only place that offered the opportunity to walk away. I could not walk on the beach and the room had been void of escape. Carefully, I took one step at a time. I could feel the narrow passage spin under my feet. My eyes played tricks on me, and many times, I could swear that everything around me was constantly shifting, moving on its own and it was I who remained stationary. I dared not touch the walls for an even greater fear of confirming that I was indeed trapped underground.

It took all of me to contain my composure, and yet, it was hysteria that drove me to continue. I could have easily fallen into a trembling mess right there on the stairs, but I had my dignity, my vanity, to maintain. The power of my ever increasing phobias besieged my senses after ten or so steps. I froze, unable to even twitch a finger. My mouth trembled and I knew that I would soon race down the steps in hysterics, or worse, faint.

Neither outcome appealed to me. I just wanted out. I was alone, with no one to help me, offer me comfort or guide me through this tribulation. There was nothing there to sustain me, and I even worried that the oxygen would give out. Yet, I pressed onward. I had to find a way out. There had to be a way out.

As I turned the first bend in the tunnel, I could hear heavy breathing and whining coming from ahead. I was excited that I might run into someone else there. I wasn't alone. I picked up my pace.

Soon, I had come across a group of people. Each one was completely naked and pale from head to toe, with thick black lines around their eyes. Some of them were missing body parts and again others had parts of their body coming out of areas God had not intended them to spawn from - fingers sprouting from their skull or ears attached to the elbow. They were groping and fondling one another and weeping. "I need love!" one whined, "Give me love!" Another would try to attend to his need, however, it was not satisfying. He was wanting love, needing love, but unable to receive the perfect love they were each looking for.

The one emotion that I had not felt from the moment I became conscious in the cave was love. I had barely been able to muster up hope. Love just simply could not be obtained and for me, feeling love did not matter. The desperation was finding an exit, not being loved. I remember love, or what I knew to be love. I had felt loved and I had loved. All I could feel now was resentment, abandonment, bitterness and regret.

The orgy that played out before me by far had been the most sordid thing I had ever witnessed. Perhaps I am in a bar and am having some sort of drug trip... but ... what am I thinking? I've never been to a bar, not a real bar, and I've never done drugs. What is this? What am I looking at?

Why did they look the way they did? Why did they look like death? Was that how I viewed love? Love is dead. Love is unobtainable.

I turned my head and closed my eyes, but I could not shut out the visions that had already imprinted themselves on my thoughts. The noise could not be silenced either. I could try to scream over them, but what good would it do? I knew they would just moan louder and my one voice would not drown out the hoard of voices that now echoed in my ears.

Suddenly I felt this surge of pride rush through my thoughts. I lorded over their pathetic situation, knowing that I had never based myself as they had.

I snorted at them. I knew that love did not exist here. In my heart I knew this as total, irrefutable fact. They will never have it, never find it, and most certainly never receive it. Even if they could figure out what perfect love was, it still remained completely out of their reach.

I shook my head, hoping that the act would unscramble the mess going on in my mind. I had to be under the influence of some drug or alcohol, though I could not remember ever doing either. I had taken some strong pain killers once that sent me into a state of mind that I particularly never want to experience again. This did not feel the same. Though my thoughts were foggy, all of this seemed too real, more real than what little I could remember of my past. All of my sensations were heightened and everything I witnessed or felt overwhelmed me.

How did I get here with these vile people? Are they really here or am I indeed hallucinating?

I pushed past them disgusted, their sweat, blood, and other bodily fluids smearing onto me as I brushed them to get by. When I touched them, they wailed even louder with agony as though my touch was poison to them. Perhaps it was.

I rounded several spirals quickly before I slowed my pace. I wanted to be out of hearing range of them before I stopped. I never stopped, but I did take each step as though it might be my last. The horror of … well of … of the glass beach, of the white room, of those people! What is going on? Have I been abducted by aliens and put in some rat maze? I wish they would learn what they need to quickly and take me back home.

Since the beginning of this, whatever this is, I particularly paid close attention to the fact that I had not seen one shadow. I continued to look. There were no shadows here. The lighting was such that it cast no shadow. I did not even have a shadow. So why could I now see shadows?

I had turned around looking back to where I had been. Two

monster shadows stood on either side of the tunnel, cast upon the walls. These shadows were in the shape of dogs, with large, sharp teeth. They had three sharp horns protruding from their skulls, and their hair seemed wiry, as though it was wet from sweat or blood. They did not make a noise, and believe me when I tell you that I strained my ears trying to even pick up their breathing but could not, though I could see their teeth, and I knew that they were silently growling at me.

These shadows, the unknown ... so much is unknown ... so far these shadows were the scariest things that I had faced. I strained my eyes trying to make out even a paw possibly protruding from around the bend, but failed to distinguish one. I turned back around, leaving the shadows behind me. Trying to forget that they were there, but knowing that they were most likely following my every step.

I listened, yet could still not make out a noise. I ignored the shadows the best I could and took my next step.

Why is all this happening to me? Who am I that this should happen to me? I am no one, just a good person, trying to do a good thing. Most of the time I succeed in doing the right thing. This sort of thing doesn't happen to people like me, or maybe this just happens to other people, not to me. I don't get lost in parallel universes, or multiple realities, or a mere cave. Why is this happening?

My mind hurt. Every thought brought a new pain. My body began to ache in various spots. Even my eyes ached. I could not focus. To make matters worse, the rock formations moved, changing shapes every couple of seconds. I could not tell if this was my mind transforming the walls or if they were indeed changing on their own. I glanced back, with the disillusioned hope that for some supernatural reason the shadows would be gone. They were still there and this time the shadows crept closer to me, so I decided to continue forward. I did not want to face what could cast those shadows.

My logic dictates that this all had to be in my head and yet I could not get around the idea that my eyes were the true deceivers, that my eyes were playing tricks on me, not my mind. Yet the mind is what interprets what I see. The confusion my eyes created for my mind equaled the growing questions of how I came to be trapped underground.

I closed my eyes and paused on the stairs. I could feel the ground moving beneath me. No, it was not my eyes. I felt nauseated and had to continue.

Was this some sick joke? Did someone bring me here and leave me to find my own way out? Where are the kidnappers? The terrorists? The psychopath? Who brought me here? Was I really in a cave or was my mind being manipulated by drugs or hypnosis or insanity? I had seen people. Had I not? Who were they? Were they real? They sounded real, looked almost real, and most certainly felt real. Was I left here to die?

I wanted to die.

Death is not the greatest adventure, nor is it something to be revered. It is an out. I needed an out and death appeared to be my only option, yet there was nothing around to assist with my only option. Though, I did feel that I could have easily been on the verge of being scared to death. I was miserable, scared and alone. So alone. So depressed. No relief. There was no relief. The psychological pain began to manifest itself physically. The desire to just die and be over with it all intensified and also manifested itself into physical pain. I hurt all over, as if I had influenza, but ten times worse. It hurt to move and it hurt worse not to move. I could throw myself down the steps and hope that my neck would break, but what if my neck does not break and the only thing I succeed in doing is breaking my leg? I would have to hobble out of here in more pain than I am already experiencing.

I will get out, won't I? One way or another, I just had to get out.

I decided that suicide would not work, not then, not without another means at my disposal or I do believe I would have tried it.

I focused my thoughts back to trying to get out, and more specifically on the lights. Possibly knowing the light source would help me find a way out. What would light up a cave with the absence of electricity? The hilarity of glow worms crossed my thoughts briefly, but the absurdity kept me from cracking even a smile, especially since my next thought was lava. This thought scared me. I tried not to think on it. Besides, it was not quite warm enough for lava, not yet. I will say that it was not cold.

Where was the light coming from? Why couldn't I reach the light? I continued down the slope, but the illumination never fluctuated, not once. Was there an end to this spiral of steps, and would it lead out of this cave? All I could do was hope, yet hope wasn't strong enough to fight back the growing insanity that arrested my heart and mind. Hope felt like a tangible being, fleeing from me, trying to escape the depression which now controlled me. All efforts to catch up with hope failed. Depression prodded me along, as though I was cattle being led to the slaughter.

# 6

# Not Alone?

As I came around the next bend of the descending trail, I stood face to face with another being. This being was not like the group. It was clothed in a perfectly white hooded robe which covered it from head to toe. I wasn't alone! Just minutes before, my body had tightened and convulsed, the air left my lungs, and an emptiness filled my heart when I assumed I had been left alone in this nightmare. And now, here is a being!

Looking upon this being before me, those sensations found no relief. In fact, I felt more afraid and more alone seeing it there. I stared at it and continued to watch as the figure floated toward me. As it approached, I saw that it had no face. A nothingness, an emptiness filled the void of the faceless, hooded being.

I suddenly realized I recognized the creature. I had seen it when I was a little girl. I had awaken in the middle of the night and looked out my window and there it was. I had been scared then and I was scared now. Like a little girl, I screamed for my family to come, not one of them came. But why should they? They weren't there. No one was there, no one except me and this form from my darkest nightmares. Instead of walking, the spirit floated toward me, but it didn't stop. Petrified, I did not move. It continued floating closer and closer, and then, it floated through me, a cold sensation shocked the nerves throughout my body. I turned around and there was nothing. The creature had vanished, nothing of its ever being there remained. Instead, the monster dog shadows moved in and I turned back around.

Again, I was physically alone, though that white figure didn't really offer me any security of a companion in the few seconds it remained in my presence. A feeling of utter fear, a fear that grips the soul and tries to twist it till there is nothing left but a mass of flesh, bone, and terror seized my being.

I trembled from the shock. Had I just seen a ghost? Was it a ghost I saw when I was a little girl? What of the group of people? They had not put the fear in me that this being had. They represented lust and counterfeit love. This creature was deception and doubt. If only I had known then that the faceless, hooded being would be the least of my worries.

# 7

# White Room

When I turned back around, I was in the room again. Standing, I could see that I was still naked and still filthy. I still could not hide, but what did it matter. I had been seen. I had been exposed. The eyes knew everything. They knew more than I knew, or at least they knew what I refused to accept, what I ignored. I pretended that the truth was not the truth.

Even then, knowing that nothing was hidden, I still would not accept the truth. The truth did not even enter my conscious thoughts. I had put up a wall that blinded and hid me from the truth, thus the truth did not exist. What existed was confusion, fear, hate and shame.

This time, I managed to force the words out. "Why are you doing this to me?"

"You are guilty!" someone shouted.

"Who are you?" I cried.

"You are guilty!" several more shouted.

"What am I guilty of? What did I do?"

"You are guilty! You are guilty!" many voices shouted.

I jumped up trying to claw at the eyes. I could not reach them. They began to laugh at me, mock me, and scream even louder my guilt.

What had I done? Suddenly shame gripped me harder than it had gripped me so far and began to encompass every cell of my being. I was shame. I huddled in a padded corner, burying my head as far as I could between my knees and my chest. I wrapped my arms over the back of my head, covering my ears the best I could. No matter how tight I covered them, I could still hear 'guilty' from the chanting voices.

I was ashamed for even living. It did not matter if I was merely guilty for telling a little white lie, I felt guilty that I had been allowed to live. I felt like a lie was equal to thievery and even murder. I was the scum of the earth, not worthy of freedom, not worthy of forgiveness, not worthy of love.

I yearned for them to just end me. Completely erase my existence. But if they killed me, is there an afterlife? I've always believed in Heaven, but I'm not good enough to go there. I deserve Hell, but do I want to spend eternity in utter suffering? I don't believe I deserve that either. I did many good things, which outweigh the few bad things I did. Is there really a Hell? They never talked about Hell in Church. They talked about Heaven.

I cried. I felt so abandoned, and yet, I felt that I had not earned the right to have company. Just end me.

My arms were aching and my neck was cramping, so I loosed my grip on my body, relaxing my muscles.

# 8

# Reality?

I was standing, though I had not gotten up. I was clothed. It was dark. It took several minutes for my eyes to adjust.

Why do I keep going back and forth? Am I in a paradox of realities? This just has to be a dream. Nothing else makes sense.

The shame I had felt still lingered, yet it was muffled by the fear this darkness brought. I could feel the growing panic. I took in a breath, but the airway had been constricted. I felt as though I was having an asthma attack. I tried to fight off the growing panic, yet calming myself proved impossible. How could anyone remain calm in a place like this? My lungs tightened, causing my inhales and exhales to increase, thus the amount of oxygen intake decreased. I panted for air. I'm not even convinced there was oxygen to breathe.

The scary thing is I did not faint from lack of oxygen. I did not die from being unable to breathe. I just continued to fight for

27

air, always fighting for air. I was tired of fighting, fighting for air, fighting for each step. I just wanted everything to end. If it meant that I would cease to exist, then so be it! But it did not end. I did not end. I continued to feel and I really did not want to.

'Why me?' I wondered. Why am I in this situation? What did I ever do to grant myself this insanity? Am I insane? Is this real? It feels real enough: the emptiness, the loneliness, the desperation for air. Am I dreaming? If I am, I need to wake up! My mind whirled through questions and fears, rationalizing and insanity. I couldn't make heads or tails of this place. I'd never heard of such a place. I'd never heard of anyone becoming lost in a cave with ghosts. In fact, I only knew of one person who even believed in ghosts, and that was only because she claimed to have seen one when she was at a haunted mansion on a college trip. I need someone to help me! God, why am I here? And where is here?

Why do we wait until we are at our lowest points to call on God? Is He only available when we cannot go on? Is He available at all? I never called on God before. I never needed Him before. He did not answer. He did not come to my help. I wanted to doubt God's existence, yet I knew He existed and knew that He was refusing to help me. I must truly be the scum of the earth.

I took in the best breath I could and walked on. Standing in one place, whining about being here, did me no good at all. I needed to find the way out.

# 9

# Deeper or Nearer

How deep is this cave? How deep is the earth? For hours I crept along. Then again, was it hours or possibly days, or minutes that felt like hours? Time itself became a paradox here. Yesterday, today, tomorrow, they are all the same. They are all now. They are all before. They all will be. Time had stopped. Time no longer existed. This place is void of time.

Can you imagine what timelessness is? It is completely unfathomable. We live in time. There is a beginning and an end to everything. I have always been here, even when I wasn't. How much sense does that make? To you, no sense at all. To me, still no sense and yet it is reality. I don't know how long I have been here, and yet, I have been here forever.

Each step of this path feels an eternity. I go on, not motivated by anything. I go on because my legs keep walking.

My mind has no control of my body. My emotions have given my body cause to respond. I should be huddled in some corner, petrified, unable to move, but I keep walking, down and down. Will power is not what moves me. I am not strong. I am weak; I am pathetic. I move because that is what I am now designed to do. I cannot stop. It is forbidden. Scientific laws have been rewritten, and one now states that Julia Chasen must keep walking down the never ending steps.

Down, deeper and deeper, further and further from the surface I traveled if there ever was a surface. I remember what the surface of the earth looked like. I remember often stopping and literally smelling the roses. Was it all a dream? It feels like a dream.

Why was I descending? I needed to ascend. But in the initial cave, the cavern that I awoke in, the start of all of this, there was only one way out: the stairs that spiraled downward. This all had to be in my mind. This stuff doesn't happen, not in real life. I wanted to stop, to sit down, and quit, but a driving force pulled me to continue on down this trail.

Nothing changed around me, and yet everything was constantly changing. Every rock face looked the same and they were all different. Am I getting close to the end? Will I find the way out? I doubted there ever existed a way out, but if there was no way out, then how did I get there? Hope, no hope, more of desperation pushed me. I had to find a way out. Where was the beach, or the room? Light? Who is this evil to put me down here?

Anger overpowered my thoughts. Hate warmed my mind. Needing a release for the ever rising rage, I screamed with all that I had, and the beastly noise spiraled down the path ahead of me. I didn't deserve this! I hated where I was at. I hated whoever put me there. Why didn't this spiral end?! I wanted to hit something. I wanted to take my frustration out on something, someone, but the fear of the shifting rocks prevented me from acting out my aggression. I was not concerned that I would break my hand or my foot by hitting or kicking the tunnel wall. I almost welcomed pain; it would take my mind off the beastly rage. No, it was a fear of knowing that by touching the wall something unpleasant would present itself. Still, the strength of the rage built up inside of me, tearing away at my morals and my sanity. A rabid beast was trying to break free from the bondage of my mind and I was having a hard time keeping it back. Fear kept it in check. But I felt, I knew, if someone had come around the corner at that moment, with the rage built up within me at that second, I would have killed them, tearing them to pieces with my bare hands, or at least desperately trying to do it.

The rage was so intense that I grabbed my arms and dug my nails into my own flesh until the pain revived my failing sanity. I looked down at my bleeding arms, the flesh hanging from the scratches I had inflicted on myself and was mortified at what I had done and that an emotion such as rage had made its way into my mind and heart. It was worse than just my mind and heart being consumed, but I could feel every pore of my being pulsating rage. Every element of me hated. I hated everyone, everything and even me. I hated what I had become. I hated that I had allowed someone to do this to me. I could not shake the rage. It became a part of me—a part that I constantly kept pushing back, which at times was easier to do as fear took its place.

I turned around, ready to battle the beasts. Their shadows were small. I could have attacked their shadows if I thought it would have done any good. Let them try to get me! The hate powered me and I felt invincible, though only for a brief second. The shadows increased in size quickly and even grew to larger than what I've seen thus far. The detailed clarity of their

31

shadows stunned me and I could even see the saliva drip from their teeth. I decided that I didn't really want to battle them at all and I returned to my descent.

As I shook my head in frustration, trying to ignore or force from my mind the constant conflict of whether I should quit or continue, I stared at the shifting wall. The hate had given me the distraction I required to momentarily ignore my fear of the tunnel walls. I watched it as it moved, and it didn't entirely appear to be made of dirt and clay but instead was made of organic matter. My eyes and my mind finally agreed that the rocky surface of the wall was moving.

I stared in horrified shock as right before my eyes a creature pulled himself from the wall of rock. I didn't know what to do, what to think, or even where to go. I just hoped that everything was only a bad dream, a dream that I would wake up from at any minute. It was all just a bad dream. It had to be. The hallucination had to stop! The drug trip needed to end! I've never taken drugs in my life, so what is all this? I wanted my eyes and mind to stop agreeing. If they did, then what I witnessed isn't real and the truth can be made known to me.

God, what is this creature? Is this of Your creation or did we really evolve from slime? This is pretty close to slime. I bet the evolutionists would have a field day with this link.

The vile mess that slumped before me didn't look human, at least, not anymore. His features hung haphazardly from his body, if one could call it a body. To me, it looked like a poor 3-D imitation of one of Picasso's abstract paintings. The Picasso limped; one leg was a foot longer than the other. As it circled me, the narrow passage expanded wide enough for both of us to occupy the space. This creature was much different from the apparition I encountered several miles above me. Confused, I tried to make sense out of how this person or thing could still move, how it came to be in its state of decomposition, why decomposition could move on its own.

I must be trapped in a bad movie. Maybe zombies really do exist. Was it going to eat me? You laugh, you mock, but you don't know the fear I felt. You don't know the confusion that refused to make order, to make sense. Zombies were just as good an explanation as any.

If only it had been a zombie.

Startled, I could hear a gurgling coming from the creature. It was trying to talk. Then suddenly, it spoke.

"So you have made it here, too," he stated or asked. I could not tell. Either way, there was forlornness in the statement.

His lips were in two different places on his body: the upper lip hung where an ear might, the lower one was planted on his chin. I couldn't figure out how he was talking to me. He reeked of decay so bad that I could taste it. I covered my nose and mouth with no success. I wanted to vomit. I needed to vomit. My body teased me as it convulsed, ready to spew up anything that was still settled in my stomach, and yet it refused to give up my last meal.

With a new terror to focus on, disgust tore at my throat. "Who are you?" I managed to ask.

Why was I talking to it? Was I that desperate not to be alone? I was extremely desperate, mockingly so, and that is what I felt—that this creature was mocking my loneliness. I was an easy target for mockery.

He looked straight into my face. His eyes were the only recognizable part of his body, and even then they stared past me. They didn't even look into my soul. His eyes made me feel as though I no longer had a soul. "I am a great healer," he boasted with perfect clarity and enunciation. If he had been able to stand straighter, let alone stand at all, he would have. It did

33

appear as though he had straightened himself a little, pulling in some of his more sluggish body parts.

If he was a great healer, then why didn't he heal himself? I guess you cannot expect much out of great healers. Maybe if he had been the best, but he clearly was not. I shook the thought from my mind. This, all of this, had to be something concocted in my mind. None of it could be real. If someone gave me some drug that is causing all of this, when I do come around, and I better come around, I'm going to kill that person.

If my mind was playing tricks on me, I could have been looking at a doctor. I might even be in a hospital or something of the like. It could explain the padded room. Maybe someone was conducting experiments on me. I never cared much for doctors, so it was plausible that my mind simply contorted the image before me so that I saw what I felt about the medical profession instead of what was actually there. Good, for the first time I had managed to rationalize the situation at hand. It still didn't seem to matter. I relaxed a bit, but the images before me remained.

I closed my eyes and tried to picture a normal medical exam room. I tried to picture a normal doctor. The images in my mind would not focus on normal. Was I going insane? The images that my mind created were almost worse than what I had been looking at, so I quickly opened my eyes. The Picasso creature had not changed. What does that mean? Am I crazy or is he real? I was determined to ignore what I saw and hope that it would get better.

Hope had just become another word, the same as box or and or nothing. Hope is not tangible. At one point in my life, the life that I cannot remember, I think that hope had been tangible. I had held it. For some reason, here, I could not hold it.

"You're a doctor? What kind?" I wanted to take back the last question. What if he responded with psychotherapist or psychologist? To my dismay or relief, he wouldn't answer with either.

His countenance changed, and in a dismal reply, he said, "I was what they called a witchdoctor, now, I'm of no consequence. And since you are here, you are of no consequence either."

What's that suppose to mean? No consequence? Witchdoctor? This man before me must be a patient. We were both suffering from delusions. I couldn't walk past him. Not without touching him, and seeing him the way he appeared to me, I couldn't possibly go near him.

He kept talking, "My life and death are worth nothing; they aren't even worth this." He waved his arms around signaling everything around him. "But, I'm here anyway."

Not worth this? There, he is right. Nothing deserves this.

Wait, did he say death? Death? If I'm crazy, I'm not *this* crazy. There was no reason why they should put me in a hall with this lunatic. He might try something. He better not come near me.

Oh, no! I glanced at the surrounding walls and watched them as they continued to move towards me. The tunnel began to narrow again, making it too small for the two of us to stand on one step. He now stood in front of me, but I wasn't watching him. I watched the walls. I took in two deep breaths. The ceiling and floor began to spin and I was losing my balance. Focus on him! Not the walls. On him.

"You're crazy. Stay away from me!" I yelled at him. I tried to take a step backward, but I couldn't. I actually picked up my foot, but moving it behind me proved impossible. It was as if I couldn't go back from where I came. I wanted to turn around to see why I could not go back, but everything below my torso would not move. I turned my head and looked out of the corner of my eye. Above me had vanished. All that remained was empty space and two shadows. "Go away! Leave me alone! Just go away!" I shouted at the Picasso and at the shadows.

I turned my head back around and closed my eyes, counted to five, and then opened my eyes again knowing that he had to be a figment of my deluded imagination and would fade into oblivion upon opening my eyes. Horror! He was still there.

An icy chill radiated from the center of my chest. How could a being as hideous as this man be real? He couldn't, yet I had seen the ghost. I must be crazier than I thought. No, I'm not crazy. I've been healthy my whole life. I've never had a case of mental instability. Maybe this is a nervous breakdown. I felt broken. What stress had I been under to warrant a nervous breakdown? Remember! Why can't I remember?

"Why am I here?" I screamed and closed my eyes again. This time when I opened my eyes the Picasso had vanished and so had my surroundings.

# 10

## Torture Chamber

I had been thinking hard on my bedroom, a room of safety. It took sweat and tears to focus my thoughts on my bedroom. When I opened my eyes, joy flooded me. I had managed to get myself out of that horrid place. My dresser, my bed, my closet were all how I remembered them to be. I stood in the middle of the room. The nightmare was over, I was awake, the sun poured in from the window, and life was good. I looked in the mirror. I was in my pajamas, and I was clean, not a spot of imperfection on me.

I stepped over to my bed and hopped in. I wanted to remain in that room for the rest of the day ... for the rest of my life. I felt safe. I curled up in my bed and pulled the covers tightly over me. I wanted to stay there.

Then I wanted to leave. My sheets took life and held me down, wrapping themselves around my whole body and binding me to the bed. What was going on now? I looked over and noticed that every mirror in my room: the full length wall mirror, my dresser mirror, even my hand mirror were all shattered. The glass then exploded from them and flew at me. My body convulsed as every shard of mirror penetrated my flesh.

The terror, the loss of blood, the demolished organs would have killed anyone. But I was still alive. I watched with one eye, the other had a huge piece of glass in it, as my pillow, without visible aid, raised and came down on my face. I was being suffocated! The shards of glass on my face were being forced in even further, cutting me even more.

Would you like me to describe the pain? How good is your imagination? Can't you imagine the pain yourself without me telling you how it felt? Have you ever been cut before? Well this doesn't compare. It's as though someone dropped you into a wood chipper, but you came out alive. Every nerve in your being is screaming, and then your face feels as though a five hundred pound person is sitting on it. Your nose breaks. Your cheek bones crack. Your tongue is in the way, so you bite it and then it gets stuck in your throat. Your neck spasms, as does your chest. Your head begins to pound and then pounds harder until you literally feel and hear your head explode.

I was dead. I felt dead. No one could have survived that torture. I wanted to be dead. In death, I would no longer feel. I would not wish to be out of the cave again as long as I could go back and not hurt, not like this. I did hurt there, but nothing as compared to here.

I felt the release of the pillow and the sheets. My body could still feel the pain, so much pain. My eyes were impossible to open: the one still forced shut by the shard of glass, the other from the eye socket breaking and part of the bone jabbing the lid down.

# 11

## What?

My eyes did finally open. I forced them open with great hesitation and pain, and once I realized I could move my arms, I felt my face. There was no glass, though I could feel moisture, a sticky residue around my eyes, my nose and mouth, most likely blood.

I cried, washing away some of the blood from my face.

I am taunted at every turn. Even when I can manage to think of some place better, and then also manage to actually go there, the place ends up being just as bad as, or even worse than, here. The cave was now home. I hated the cave. God, end this!

I never prayed so much in my life. I wanted … oh, who cares what I wanted? No one cared. God certainly did not care. Why was I being tortured? I was never bad enough to deserve this. In fact, I was a good person. I obeyed the law. I went to church when I had time. I helped people, so why would God allow this? There must not be a god after all. Maybe I was a part of the wrong religion, perhaps someone else's gods were real.

Looking down at the stairs below me and no longer boxed in by the medicine man, I stepped forward. Rocks closed in all around me. It almost seemed that it was not my phobia causing the walls to close in, but the frightening fact that they were indeed moving in on my every step. I would definitely find myself deserving to be in this crazy hellhole if I didn't find my way out and soon—I am already on the brink of insanity, seeing things that should not be. I should be able to find my way out. I used to have a great sense of direction. Yet, for the first time in my existence, there is only one direction to take, and due to my logical sense of direction, I knew that going down should not be the direction to take.

To prevent myself from going mad over knowing that I should be heading up instead of down, my new focus was to find the light source. Science tells us, or possibly common sense, that if there is a light, there is a source for that light. Where is this illumination coming from? The dimness grew less the deeper I went, and for a moment I believed I could almost sense a hint of hope that there was indeed a way out and I was closing in on it. Would it not get brighter the closer I came to a source of light? I tried to expect to see the light source and soon. I also tried to expect that the light source was the outside: sun and sky. Being in the dark made it hard to expect, let alone hope.

My mind lost focus, as my eyes were distracted by the walls again. I came to notice oddities in the stone walls. The rocks seemed to be sedimentary, but some of the pieces of sediment were much more pronounced than others. I decided to stop and inspect it further. Staring hard at the wall, I discovered that the white sections in the rock were bones. I dared not touch the walls themselves, but the ivory pieces did appear to have once been the skeletal makeup of humans! The knowledge of walking through death produced a cold sweat to breakout all over me. I was freezing and sweat poured out from every pore of my body. I felt dizzy. I was going to faint, and yet, I was cursed to remain conscious. I didn't understand any of it.

A wave of heat knocked into me, drawing my attention away from my unanswered questions and the boney walls. The sweat evaporated within seconds of being produced. The suffocating heat prevented me from producing any further sweat. One moment I was freezing, though not because it was actually cold, and the next I was overwhelmed with temperatures that could evaporate a lake in seconds.

It was always warm. The cold I experienced had been produced internally—it would not happen again. I wish it would. It is so hot.

From past experiences, I noticed that the deeper one ventured into a cave, the colder the atmosphere became. That wasn't so for this one. The temperature climbed higher the farther down I went. My concentrated purpose was to get out, which alone gave me strength and perseverance to walk on. But now, a fearful thought popped into my head, what if I was heading into the mouth of a volcano? What if right behind these walls was lava? Where else would the heat come from? It could explain the bones. Didn't they used to sacrifice people to volcanoes or is that only in the movies?

I felt so afraid and alone. What was going on with my mind? I could see the shadows on the wall beside where I stood. The monsters had crept up while I stood there investigating the bones. I stumbled ahead, determined to keep ahead of them.

# 12

## What Now?

If teleportation were a reality at this moment in time, I just experienced it. This was different from the other places I had been. The other times, I had been focused on somewhere else, even the padded room I had desired to be in a safe environment and then I was, or for a moment it felt safe. But this was different. I had not been thinking of anything except the possibility of a volcano. I've never liked volcanos, so the thought of being in one caused me to panic. My focus had been fear of being melted.

Quicker than a blink, I found myself on a bed in a hospital being rolled down a hallway. The blurry figures around the bed wore doctor and nurse uniforms. People! Real people. "It's going to be okay, Mrs. Chasen. We're going to take real good

43

care of you," one of them said to me. The lights above my head hurt my eyes, but I didn't care. It was light! The walls were cement painted in white. No rocks! No darkness! No bones! And no heat! An air conditioning vent briefly blew a cool breeze across my body. I tried to talk, but the disorientation I felt prevented me to even make sense of what was happening. I closed my eyes and then . . .

# 13

## How?

I was back in the cave! Why?! I spun around just to make sure I really was back. I only glimpsed the shadows, which were farther up the steps. Rock, steps, dimness, heat, bones—I hated it. With great passion I hated this place, and the hate increased with each second I remained there.

I wanted to go back to the hospital. I wanted to be with people, and even with the amount of discomfort I felt for doctors and hospitals, I was ready to spend the rest of my life with them. Anywhere but here!

"I want out of this place! Dear God, help me!"

A waterfall of tears burst from my eyes like a busted dam. I had to still be in the hospital, right? I looked at my clothes; I wore a pair of jeans and a t-shirt. Nothing could be found in my pockets. Nothing made sense. If I were in the hospital, wouldn't I be wearing a gown, even a medical bracelet? But, I wasn't. Right now, two and two did not make four. Three or five, but not four.

What is reality? What is the point of reality? Does reality exist to the crazed? Does reality exist at all? Is this an alternate dimension? Did I take a wrong step and walk through a portal to an alternate reality? Where is here? What is here? Does here even exist? Or is it all an illusion, something my crooked mind distorted just to torment me? I would much rather be there instead of here. Take me back!

My life before ... was it all a dream? Did I make it all up in my mind? My family ... my friends ... were any of them real? Are they real? My job, my daily activities, everything, all of it seems like a distant thought, a forgotten dream. They no longer seem real and yet they were very real every moment I was a part of them. Now, this life, if this can be considered living, is more real than I care to conceive. I would rather be wiped from existence than continue residing here. I wish I had never existed, and I don't even care if my children had never existed, rather than being here now. In fact, I would gladly change places with any one of my children. No, what am I thinking! How could I think that? But how true the statement is! I hate myself for saying it, for agreeing with it, but with all my heart, I would ... I would change places with one of my dear children, my husband, my parents, my siblings, with anyone as long as I could get out of this ... out of this HELL!

I was a good person. I am a good person. Bad things shouldn't happen to good people, at least, not such an evil as this. I've worked hard all my life. I worked hard helping people when I could, giving of myself, time, and monetarily. How could I have been treated like this? Dropped into a cave and sealed in! Or going insane! Maybe if I hadn't been doing so

46

much for others, if I hadn't worked so hard to be good, then I wouldn't have gone crazy. I wouldn't be here! I would at least feel justified had I lived my life in promiscuity, waging war, hurting others, indulging myself. Why am I here?

Shame hit me again, taking over the other emotions that waged war within me. I hated myself. I deserved even worse than this. I slapped my face. What was I thinking? Fear took over, depression not far behind. I had sunk to the lowest depths. If this wasn't hell, I never wanted to go there.

Who wants to go to hell? I used to hear 'meet you in hell' all the time. Why would anyone want to go to some place worse than this? I also used to hear 'go to hell.' Why would anyone wish for anyone to go there? I wouldn't wish it, and yet, I would also trade places with everyone on earth just to be out of this place. My emotions and thoughts continuously contradicted themselves. I felt evil. I felt possessed. Was I really wanting pain and suffering to come upon people I once loved? Don't I still love them? I don't know what love is. I'm a vile creature.

Desperation can be an ugly thing.

Why am I here? Where is here? Have I asked those questions already? I can't remember. What happened to the witchdoctor? Where did he go? Did he slip back into the wall? Will I end up as part of the mass of bone sediment pressed into the walls of this tunnel? No one would answer my questions. I kept most of them to myself, fearing to utter them, fearing to give life to the words, fearing of causing the very thing I did not want to be true – that all of this was real.

I reluctantly continued down. There was nothing but rock around me: above, beside, below. The empty space, occupied only by me, seemed to be even emptier with me walking through it. I felt that my presence did not fill the void, but instead brought a stamp of hollowness to the cave. I felt emptier than the cave.

Where was the light coming from?

I decided that I needed to refocus my thoughts again. Distractions plagued me. My mind could not focus on any one thing for more than a matter of seconds. Redundancy mocked my questions. "Ahhh!" I screamed in frustration.

I was beginning to sound insane. No ... I had been sounding insane for a while, too long of a while... I am crazy. Crazy is here. This place is crazy. This place is that part of one's mind that one finds themselves when they go mad. They become trapped here. This place does not just embody insanity, it is insanity. If you were to look at a picture of crazy, if crazy was something you could see, you would be looking at a picture of this place.

My nerves were all on edge and I experienced trembles as I continued. Uncontrollable spasms erupted all over my body. Was I having a seizure? How long would it last? Don't people die from seizures? Am I dying?

I didn't fall on the floor and I was completely aware that I was trembling. After my fear that I was having a seizure passed, I changed my mind and believed that I was having yet another nervous breakdown. How many nervous breakdowns can one have? Can one have a breakdown within a breakdown? Because that is exactly how I felt.

I heard voices ahead. Maybe they could help? I rushed toward them. They could help me. I knew they could show me the way out. Even with the knowledge that those of whom I had come across so far here were of entirely no use to me, I held that there was a possibility that there was at least one that could. Or perhaps, they were stuck down here, too. I slowed my pace with that revelation. Maybe no one knew the way out. I cannot think like that. I have to grasp to what little hope I can find within myself and hold tight. Once hope is lost, everything is pointless. Wasn't hope already lost?

*How?*

The voices became clearer and louder and I knew I had almost reached them. I was descending too deep. I needed to ascend to get out. At least, that is what the logic of my mind believed to be true. Do you get out of a hole by crawling to the bottom or by climbing to the top?

# 14

## A Crowd

Suddenly my feet carried me to a crowded church building. There were people in the aisles, lining the pews, and leaning against the walls. The stage was full of people in robes. How did I get there? I turned around and kept shaking my head in disbelief. I did not recognize the church. I had never been there before. I don't understand. Why this church?

The preacher started in, but all he did was wave his hands around. Not one word from his lips was audible. He even got red in the face, yet silence was all that followed. The people weren't even trying to pay attention. Their eyes and manners betrayed their hearts.

Suddenly I realized that I could see right through each

person. Literally see through their physical body. There was a huge hole in everyone, including the preacher, and it revealed that not one of them had a heart. They were empty. As I continued to stare at them, I noted that the lighting in the church began to dim and the people began to dry up. Their flesh was being sucked dry of all moisture, the emptiness had consumed them, and they were a pile of dried bones.

When the church, too, had faded, I stood in a cave with empty people. The church had never been there. The cave had been here the whole time. I had been given a glimpse of their reality. Such an empty existence. Why was I being shown this? What relevance did this have on my life? The voices had come from this cave, the voices I had been chasing, hoping to find, hoping for guidance, hoping for a way out, they became silent. The emptiness had stolen their voices also. They had nothing left but hollow, dry bones. Their bones shattered and they became part of the dusty path I stood on.

I could suddenly hear their voices once more. Though their bodies were dust their spirit remained and they cried out. "It's not fair. I didn't know." I could hear the pain in their voices, physical pain, pain compared to no other. I wanted to grieve for them, but I couldn't. Before this cave, before the darkness, I would have felt sorry for them, but now, who cares? It bothered me that I did not care, that I could not care, and yet my only focus was me and how I was going to get out of there. Besides, they deserved what they got. They were empty, how could they even feel?

# 15

## Downward On

I walked past the bone dust, past the voices. My feet felt as though I was walking on the beach of broken glass barefoot. When I looked down to investigate, I found my shoes were drenched in a dark, tarry residue. I must have stepped in tar, I imagined. On pausing and bending over to check my shoe closer, I could smell the iron and realized that it was not tar but blood.

My shoes were coated in blood ... no, they are bleeding. My shoes are bleeding! I pulled back the tongue of the shoe and saw my foot. It had been rubbed raw. I wanted to sit down, rest my feet and take off my shoes, but I didn't want to touch the ground. I didn't want to touch the walls. If I did, it would confirm one way or the other whether I really was in a cave or if my mind was playing tricks on me. I felt little comfort being naive or playing stupid, but I could not face the discomfort of knowing the truth. The pain felt real and that was enough for me.

Maybe it doesn't matter how good or bad you are. Maybe no matter what, you'll end up here. I'm not going to say where here is. Here is a state of mind. It can't be real! I don't want it to be real. This story will get out and they'll say it's fiction; they'll say it's just a story. But, it's not! I'm here.

No! I mustn't think like that. This is fake. None of it is real. I can't let it be real. Perhaps if I am able to convince myself that the truth is that all of this is fake, it would be. But convincing myself that all this is not real grows harder and harder the farther down into the pit I go.

The heat had increased even more and the intensity of it overwhelmed me. It burned my skin. It burned through my clothes. I am overwhelmed by the excruciating pain of each step as though I am walking on the tips of blades, and every joint in my feet and legs grows so stiff it feels as though I am shattering bone each time I put one foot in front of the other, merely to walk.

The result of this pain steals my focus from my thoughts that this world is bogus. The idea that all this is a conjuring of my own imagination fails to prevail. The pain wins and I am beginning to accept where I am. But I don't want to be here. I cannot imagine why I would be here. I will be stuck in here forever! Forever is a very long time. Forever is the absence of time … eternity … no beginning and no end.

Wasn't I supposed to be focusing on the light? "Stay focused! Do you want to stay here forever? Don't you want to find a way out?" I asked myself.

The light did increase, little by little. It was still dark, darker than even moonlight. I used to be sensitive to light, preferring the dark. Now, I would take on the sun for some light.

The heat was just unbearable. I wanted to vomit, my stomach churned enough, but I could find no relief. My skin could not even sweat. My blood had to have turned to powder. I was probably a walking skeleton of dry bones. I was glad there were no mirrors, though even then, I wasn't trying to impress anyone. I just wanted out.

Around the next bend, I could see the entrance of a side cavern. Was it a way out?

With the possibility of finally finding a way out, I did not hear the noise that came from the cavern until I was a few steps away from the entrance. That noise was another boot in my face, another kick to my side. I knew it would not be an exit, but I didn't expect what I saw.

As I made my way closer, the separate cavern to my left rained with music. I inched slowly, not wanting to be discovered by whoever made the noise. When I built up the nerve to peek in, I saw a man charred, burnt beyond all recognition. Smoke still rising from parts of him, yet I knew he had been killed long enough ago that there should have been no more smoke. I don't know how I knew. I just knew.

There was something about the cave, something that gave me insight to everything and everyone around me, that is, if I allowed my mind to go there. Most of the time I ignored the revelations, the knowing. It creeped me out. I knew how people felt. Every sense within me amplified till I could know their thoughts, hear the pain screaming from the tunnel walls, know all the evils that resided there. I knew everything, the whole truth the second I became aware of that place, but I ignored it, fought it off. The truth sometimes hurts and this time the truth down right terrified me.

Upon further gawking, I was stunned to conclude that the song was coming from this charred man. He moved! He belted out from his lips the lyrics to a song. He had to be dead and yet, he was singing. I couldn't make out all the words but of those that I could many were obscenities and slurs. The song promoted rape and murder, hate and lust. I didn't listen to the rest. I was appalled at the lyrics. I was appalled at him. Didn't he have the decency to 'rest in peace,' to die with silence on his lips?

I could stand it no longer. I knew he couldn't hurt me. "Shut up!" I screamed at him, overcome by the passion of my desire to silence him by merely yelling at him. "Scream in pain, but shut up with that pointless song!" I added to no avail.

His song continued with suicide, treating your best friend like the enemy, and so forth. When I slipped past the cavern, he didn't even notice me. He just continued. I couldn't understand why? I could not understand anything. Why won't my brain shut up? Why won't my brain end this disillusion?

The monsters' shadows had snuck into the cavern without my notice until I saw them on the wall behind the man. He had not noticed them. I could not tear my eyes away due to the rising curiosity that consumed me. I wanted to look away. I wanted to run away. I did not want the shadows to catch up to me, so I could only imagine what they were about to do to him.

Suddenly, the shadows leapt from the wall and were a solid mass, a dark shadowy mass, which stood on either side of the man. He still sang, not seeing them, or just ignoring them. The beasts opened their mouths. I could see the carnivorous teeth, dripping with saliva, and then they fell upon him, tearing what flesh was left off his arms and torso. He cried out, but the screams were still with his lyrics upon his lips. It was as though his music was his god and he was crying out, pleading for help, but the words could do nothing for him.

I turned and faced the tunnel. I could not help him. I didn't want to, but I did want to get out of there before the monsters decided that raw meat would taste just as good as the well done man they were now devouring.

I walked on, feeling as rotten as his song. It took many steps and several spirals before I could no longer hear his sickening voice. I used to listen to music to help lift my spirit. I wanted to feel better, and music helped lighten the mood. It was therapeutic and often an escape from the madness around me. The music here brought no such escape, no peace, no joy, and most certainly did not keep me from the madness. In fact, the music only proved further that I was mad. From having to listen to his music, I felt worse and wanted to die…

# 16

## Where?

As I rounded a jutting rock, the lights had increased immensely. I blinked my eyes trying to adjust to the glare. When I could finally see, I found myself in a hallway with a row of doors on either side of me. Bleach and a mixture of medications permeated the air and filtered into my olfactory sense. The increase of oxygen clouded my focus and I felt overwhelmingly tired. Why . . . no how did I arrive here?

How am I able to be in one place and then immediately step into another so completely different, and yet, just as torturous? How does it keep happening? Why does it keep happening? Is this really possible, to jump from reality to reality, or is this still all in my mind? I may not be able to remember everything, at least the reason for me ending up here, but I cannot accept that my mind would be this disturbed to create these multiple hells. So my question remains, what is this?

Was this hallway real? To find out the answer, I fell to the floor. It was easier to fall to the floor than to slowly kneel, as the pure oxygen that filtered into my lungs and spread through me sent my head into a fog. I stopped my descent once I made it to my knees. I dropped my hands to the ground. It felt real. The cold surface was quite welcome to my sore skin, my sore body. I wanted to melt into the floor and become one with it. I could spend the rest of my existence as part of the floor with people walking upon me as long as I did not have to leave that moment. A single moment where I did not burn, fear for my life, or ache with excruciating pain. To be a floor!

Still on my knees and having rested on my forearms with my head in my hands as I tried to steady the spinning hallway, I slowly sat up, dragging my arms off the floor. I didn't want to look at my arms. I feared that this … well, what appeared to be a hospital … the same place I have found myself in once before, might just be fake.

I did look. My body felt numb, so I had to look. After minutes of just kneeling there, I lifted my forearms so that I could see the side of them that had rested on the floor. In the tunnel, I had been very afraid to touch the ground beneath me or the walls, for fear of something dreadful happening. Here, I only feared that it might all be an illusion.

Relief pounded through my body when I could clearly see that my arms were intact. Acid had not burned the skin, nor had insects eaten away at them. Just to be sure, I crawled to the wall and leaned against it. Slowly I climbed my hands up the wall, and slowly I ascended until I stood. Taking a look at my hands once I was erect, I kissed the palms when I saw that they, too, were unharmed.

I needed to find someone, anyone who could help me, who would help me. Sluggishly, I slowly jogged down the hall, looking through the windows of the doors on either side of me. I could see empty beds, empty offices, and empty labs. None of the computers and equipment seemed to be on, though the lights overhead were brightly lit. The building appeared to be abandoned, or at least, not in use. Now that I could see, there was nothing to see. I could not find one person. I was alone, still alone.

I went in search of the nurses' station, hoping that I could find some answers there. I don't know what made me think that nurses would be on duty when there were no patients or doctors present. Either way, I had decided that there was a remote possibility that there would be a nurse on duty and that he or she could help me. I just first had to find the station. I turned down a hall which offered as good a chance as any in locating a nurses' station.

I was almost running by this point trying to find someone, anyone. I was so tired of being alone. I was tired of needing help and not getting any. I helped so many people and now when I need them, not one of them is around. I felt the hate creeping into my thoughts, my heart being consumed by derision. See if I ever help anyone ever again. I will show them. When I get out of here, I will tell everyone 'no' and do things for myself.

Ahead of me a set of double doors read 'Emergency.' As I approached the double doors and reached out my hands to grab the handles to open them, a thunderous roar boomed from behind the doors, forcing my hands to drop immediately. In the pit of my being, I knew I needed to get out of there before the owner of the beastly roar found me. Had I any grain of curiosity before I heard that ghastly roar, I was then cured from what killed the cat.

The lights in the hall began to flicker. I stepped backward, and for the first time in the nightmare, I found that I could move backwards. Perhaps I was no longer dreaming and this was finally reality. But again, what is this? Slowly, I turned and quickened my pace. In a couple of steps, I began at a slow run. I turned my head to look behind me. The set of lights nearest the Emergency Room went out. I ran onward, keeping in the light. Another roar vibrated the walls and floor and I could hear the double doors burst open and slam closed. I glanced back and only saw that the lights were shutting off behind me. I ran toward the lights that remained on. I was nearing the end of the hall toward another set of double doors that read exit. Another roar concluded with the last set of lights shutting off and leaving me in the dark...

# 17

## How?

I waited and waited for the beast to attack me. I wondered if it was another one of the shadow monsters. I could see nothing in the darkness, however I could hear, and I heard nothing. Then a moan and muffled screams in the far distance broke the silence. My eyes had finally adjusted to the dark and I saw the orange glow.

Had I really been in a hospital or had I been here the whole time? What is real? Who or what is tampering with my mind? Is it my mind or am I really being transported back and forth between realities? What is the truth? Can anyone tell me? Will anyone tell me, or am I forced to ask these questions for all eternity?

The anger I felt before taunted me. I hated everyone I had

ever helped. Why would they allow this to happen to me? Why are they not here helping me? Why am I here alone? Where is my husband? Where are my children? Why did I slave all those years, helping so many people, only to end up here alone? To add insult to injury, I hurt all over. There is not one part of my body that does not ache. My body was on fire, and my nerves were all inflamed.

I shook my head. No! This all has to be in my mind. Just shut my mind off. I want this reality to end.

How can a perfectly healthy individual develop acute dementia in a short period of time? Is this a short period of time? ... I don't remember! ... Can I be demented while I wonder if I've totally lost all sense? ... What happened to me? ... What happened to me?!

Perhaps I suffered some great tragedy or traumatic event? ... What happened? ... Think! Focus!

I focused my thoughts on what I could remember. My head throbbed as I struggled to remember. Nothing! My mind was a blank. This can't be real; none of it. My mind is trapped in this nightmare and I can't get out. The longer I'm here, the more my previous life seems like the dream. Somehow, something happened to me and I am in a place that is causing me great stress and my confounded mind is creating this hell to continue torturing me with. If whatever traumatic event wasn't enough for me, let's just add hell to the picture.

Though I have rationalized every detail, I'm still here. Trapped, but in what? A nightmare? My mind? A real cave with scary images? Hell? My frustration has tainted my heart. Bitterness and anger control the strings as puppet masters of my emotions. The changing rocky walls manipulate and dictate my course through this maze toward God knows what. Does God even know? If this is Hell, then why am I here? I can't understand any of it.

I tried to take a step backward to no avail. I knew it wouldn't work before I even tried. Positive thinking is useless here. It is constantly thwarted by unsuccessful actions and disappointing consequences. Hope cannot be found. It is lost or was never even allowed to enter this place. Forward was my destiny. I hated forward.

Then again, going backward was hardly a way out. I would immediately run into those monsters and the same thing that had happened to that charred man would happen to me. I wasn't quite ready to be eaten. I was depressed, and I wanted to die, but I was more afraid than either.

I used to think I knew what fear was. There had been moments that sheer terror gripped my senses, but here, the amplification of fear, of terror, recreated the cell structure, the atoms of one's being, causing them to become fear. You no longer felt fear; you became fear. I've probably told you all this before, or perhaps I will tell you all this again, as I've said, time does not exist here. I am just trying to get the point across. It is important that you understand that this could happen to you. And yet, I don't really care if this happens to you. Would you like to change places? I would gladly take on whatever you are facing everyday just to get out of here. Whatever you are going through, believe me, your hell cannot compare to this one.

Step by step, I'm drawn deeper and farther into the abyss below. I move with little desire, less emotion, and no hope. A snail could beat me down the steps at my dragging speed. I don't want to move, but I can't help it. Something here won't let me stand still. It hurts to move, but it hurts even more to stop.

The fragments of bones are no longer fragments, but skulls, legs, arms, feet, hands, torsos, whole skeletons. Skin and hair mixed with the sediment in the rock. The cave walls continued to reshape themselves over and over and over, as if they were alive, or perhaps growing. My claustrophobia became mixed with so many other fears that the closing walls around me quickly became the least of my worries, and yet, continued to toy with my nerves with great success.

Around and around, the spiral never ended. Worse than motion sickness, the twirling of the stairs made even my eyes throb and I wished I could pull them out. A couple of times I even attempted it. I could see the blood under my nails, and I did not need a mirror to know that I left claw marks around my eyes.

I felt as though I was on an escalator, walking against the direction of the moving stairs. Upon looking down, I could prove this to be the case. The floor moved like the walls, though the motion of the floor appeared more like the crawling of billions of ants. And, if I had paused long enough, the insects would have been able to crawl onto my shoes, so I did not investigate the creepy crawlers that I treaded on. I ignored the crunching sound of each step and the sticky ooze that stuck to the soles of my shoes.

I could vaguely remember a time when someone asked me if I lost one of my senses which one would I most not mind losing. I cannot tell you now what I answered then, however, now ... now I wish I didn't have a single sense. I would gladly give up touch, hearing, seeing, smelling and even taste. The putrid air tasted of vomit and bile. The constant earsplitting screams refused to make me deaf. Every cell in my body exploded with stinging pain, and all I could see was darkness and a damnable orange light that tortured me.

I cried again. I screamed in pain, joining the pathetic chorus around me. To see a tree, a flower, a lake, I would give anything to see a chair.

# How?

I could hear his screams several spirals up. Descending slowly, I dreaded coming upon him, knowing that I would face agony itself. The moans of a thousand voices echoed off the cave walls and beat against my eardrums. My heart pounded and my head throbbed with the sporadic rhythm of the noise. His voice sang out above the others. "The pain! Make it stop! Please, make it stop! It hurts! I want it to stop hurting! There's no end!" he shouted clearly. The pain he suffered could be heard in his screams. I hurt with him, though I didn't need him to feel pain. I felt plenty on my own.

I saw his feet first. They were blue from cold. He dared to stretch himself on the floor of the cave, and just as I had feared, insects, like acid, ate at his flesh. Crunched in the fetal position, he continued to wail. "It was supposed to end when I pulled the trigger. The pain was supposed to end! I shot the pain right out of me! Why do I still hurt?" I inspected him and the indicated area closer to see what he was referring to, and sure enough, a bullet hole could be seen through his neck. To be in so much pain to attempt suicide only to fail, or had he succeeded? If he had succeeded then I was looking at … what … his ghost? So he's dead. He had hoped to end it all and then learn that instead of death – which for him should have meant no more existence – and yet instead he lived on with that very pain, but worse yet, stuck in this place. I wanted to feel sorry for him, but all my pity was used up on me.

I callously stepped over him and continued on. He didn't even bother to reach out to me for help. It was as though, he'd been through this all before. Though I supposed he might not have even seen me. Just because I could see him does not conclude that he would see me. He wasn't shouting at me. I just happened to be there to hear him.

The emptiness inside of me grew. I struggled to get a breath. My heart was stone. I didn't even reprimand myself for not caring about the poor man in pain. I didn't care, that I didn't care. It was his fault for being here, not mine. I hadn't pulled the trigger for him. I hadn't even caused the initial pain which caused him to be here in the first place. In truth, I hated him as much as I hated everything else here.

I struggled for another breath.

# 18

# A Way Out

A bright light just ahead of me flooded the cave. This light actually cast shadows. The excitement grew and I thought I almost felt hope, though I was not sure if I could remember what hope felt like. Either way, I thought I felt hope, something of which I thought I had lost forever.

Have I mentioned that this place is deceitful? When one thinks they feel hope, all they really feel is confusion. Their thoughts cannot make sense of the situation, so they become confused. They believe they can feel a positive emotion, yet all they are really feeling is a counterfeit or a false emotion. Their understanding of peace, hope, joy or love has been manipulated and hardened so that they can no longer feel these emotions. So when I say I felt hope, know that hope is far from what I truly feel.

I could still see the light ahead. It grew brighter with each step as I neared it. A way out at last! I'm free! I turned the bend and saw an opening. The tunnel had ended and I ran out of the cave and into the sunlight. I was outside looking at a barren land. There were no trees, no grass, no plant or animal life of any kind. The ground was dusty. I had the sun, but even that felt barren. I wondered out of the cave for this?! Am I out of the cave or is this another illusion?

You are probably tired of me questioning what is real. I, too, am tired of the same question: what is illusion, hallucination, or real? If I had an answer to this question, then possibly, most likely, I would stop asking this question. Then again, I know the answer and am choosing to ignore the answer because it doesn't fit with what I already knew to be true. The answer is completely contrary to what I believe, thus I will not, can not accept it. So I keep asking, expecting that at some point I will receive a different answer that will fit my own understanding, my own beliefs.

I stared at the barrenness. How empty it was. I was still alone. Nothing! Dust and dirt. I might as well be stuck on the moon. I didn't try to stop the outburst that erupted out of me.

"God, I hate You! Why me? Why here? What is here? Where is here? How could a loving God allow this to happen to me, to a good person? What did I ever do to You? I don't deserve this! My worst enemy doesn't deserve this! Are You listening up there?" I shouted toward the sun. "I thought You loved everyone. Why could You allow this to happen? What is wrong with me?"

I waited for an answer, and while I waited the anger within me continued to boil, continued to grow. I hated God. Why would He allow this to happen to me? Why wouldn't He hear me? Why wouldn't He answer? Perhaps, He is answering and I just cannot hear Him.

"Make me hear You!" I shouted just in case it was me with the problem, though I doubted it was me.

I obviously did something wrong to warrant this treatment, though for the life of me, I could not think of what I did that was so bad, so evil for God to turn His back on me.

The silence was unbearable. In what I had expected to be freedom, I felt trapped and alone. I fell on the ground. I didn't care anymore. Let the insects eat me. I huddled in a fetal position and cried until I was tired … well, more tired … and then I cried some more. The sun was cold. Had the world come to an end? Was I really the last to know about it? I could see forever and nothing was there.

Sulkily, I stood and turned around. I was in the tunnel, facing the abyss below. Darkness had encompassed me once more. I understood that even if I could see, there was nothing to see. The darkness only hid the emptiness, masking it, deceiving me that there might be something here to see. I didn't even bother crying. I felt too empty.

I had wanted out. I wanted out so bad that I could have dug a hole in the wall of the tunnel had I a shovel or even a spoon. I wanted out, only to find that out was just as bad as in. With the light, the emptiness could be seen, the loneliness was visible, and understanding crushed confusion. I think I would have preferred to remain confused.

I don't want this! I didn't want to be alone. I was alone, so utterly alone. I didn't want to be afraid. I was so terrified. I didn't want to hurt. I would happily die to end this agony.

My heart turned cold. No … it had been cold all along. I just now noticed how icy my chest was. Remembering the empty people, having seen right through them, I wanted to see my own heart, see if I still had one.

I placed my hand between my breasts, and then dug my fingers in. It proved to be easier than it probably should have been. I already decided I was crazy and this was merely an illusion my mind created for my undelighted benefit. I felt something hard within my chest and proceeded to pull it out from the hole I had dug into my own body. A rock rested in my hand, blood dripping from it. I had pulled a rock from my body! I screamed and dropped it.

Fate would not allow me to leave the rock behind. I was not allowed to continue with a physical void. I could only continue with a tangible emptiness. I could only continue cold. The rock rose from the ground, spinning faster than the earth. It stopped until it was level with my chest. Then it flew straight back into me with such force my body hit the invisible wall behind me that prevented me from going back. I had to carry the cold weight. It was my due.

# 19

## Still Trapped

Another noise around the next spiral set my protective instincts into action. These instincts would soon be completely removed from me. I've already said that my heart is stone. I can prove it, too. I've seen it. Held it. Nothing more than a rock, a lifeless rock. But I told you that already didn't I?

I heard a little girl screaming, "Help! Help!"

I ran around the bend and came upon a girl in a dirty, flowery, knee-length dress. Apart from the slits in her wrists and a cord around her neck, she seemed sincerely innocent. How could anyone do such a thing to a little child? Though, even that idea of innocence ended when I looked at what she held in her hand. A knife clutched in her hand and a dark goop dripped from its blade.

I should have realized that innocence does not exist here. Why would it? Nothing here is innocent. Not even I am completely innocent, though I know I'm not as bad as others. Others have done far worse things than I have. I am innocent of bloodshed, and yet I am just as guilty as this little girl before me now.

She couldn't have been more than eight or nine. Dark circles around her eyes only transformed the black pupils surrounded by bloodshot whiteness to appear that much more enraged than the rest of her appearance. The knife, which was held high as if to strike, came down hard into a person I had not even noticed being there the second before. A woman suddenly appeared, half of her body totally void of skin, exposing the blood vessels, muscle and tissue. She was stretched out on a step at the girl's feet and now had a knife plunged into her head.

The little girl looked up at me and yanked the knife back out. The woman moaned and rolled over; her eyes, filling with tears, fought back disgust and rage. She had multiple stab wounds to her torso, any of which would have killed a normal human being, but the blow to her head should have certainly ended her. The woman was still alive! After all of that, and the woman's suffering did not end.

I could see a resemblance between the woman and little girl. They were clearly mother and daughter. I stared at the wild child, watching the knife she held. Her grip on it had purpose. She knew what she wanted to do with it and I could see it in her eyes that she meant to do exactly what she wanted.

This woman's own daughter was a murdering psychopath. The woman spoke, chanting some sort of curse over her demon child. Was the child always a psychopath or had her mother made her one? My stony heart could not even break. I felt neither empathy nor apathy. I felt nothing, though possibly shock and fear, and yet, I had almost expected to see just this very situation before it happened.

She was unnaturally strong for a little girl. Again, I tried to take a step backward. I couldn't. She charged at me with the knife, with clinched teeth growling. I braced myself for the impact. With force, the knife thrust into my stomach and kept going. The girl and knife ran straight through me without leaving a physical mark. I could feel the pain of the knife ripping right through me, but I would never be able to prove it happened. There were no marks, no blood, only the pain.

The woman sunk into the stairs before me. I gazed at the steps. Why am I being forced to see this? Is this some sort of intervention technique? I don't want it! I'll change just don't show me this ever again! Did some psychopath hypnotize me to visualize these horrors?

"What do you want me to do?" I shouted. "Tell me! Tell me! For God's sake, tell me!"

I needed to get out of there. I didn't want to step where the woman had been for fear that the same thing would happen to me that had happened to her. I didn't want to sink into the earth. Where did she go? What was beneath me? Creeping along the wall, I almost braced the rocks but realized what I was about to do at the last second. I didn't want to touch the walls. Bad things would happen if I did. Bare skin against any of the rock surfaces would only bring bad things.

I sound superstitious, and I don't care. If it was you here instead of me, you would believe … more than that … you would know the same thing—don't touch the walls.

After I felt I had passed the area where the woman and little girl had been, I moved back to the middle of the passage. The middle offered a little security. The middle felt a little less scary. I was terrified beyond insanity, but in the middle, I almost felt that I might gain back some rational thought.

I couldn't rationalize the woman and the child. As hard as I tried, I could not. How would one go about explaining what I just witnessed? Understanding was a loss to me. Rational thought brought me to two conclusions: the first—I could not accept, the second—I had to be crazy. So, to ignore my rational thinking, I ran. What else could I do? I ran as hard as I could down each step, stumbling a couple of times, but not falling, until I reached a point where I had to rest. Yet, rest could not be truly found, not in that place.

I panted for air, my lungs burned. My chest pounded as my overworked heart pumped hard to keep up with me. I could even feel my face pulsating. My head ached from the pressure I had put on my lungs and heart. I was dehydrated, with no water. I could feel the blood in my veins turn to dust as the last remnants of moisture dried up. I coughed, and continued coughing until my body just wouldn't allow me to keep coughing.

# 20

## Noise

Muffled voices became clearer as I rounded my way down. Soon I was able to make out distinct phrases. The voices were many, thousands, tens or even hundreds of thousands, or even more echoed all around me. The vibration of the voices caused the walls of the tunnel to shake. The dust and bone fragments bounced on the ground and the ceiling threatened to collapse as particles floated down from it. I saw no one, but I could hear all their voices.

"The end of life will happen in 1989!"

"I am the Messiah!"

"Our new president is the anti-Christ!"

"You belong to God. You can drink this poison and not die!"

"God told me to tell you that we should be together!"

"Your glory is your hair!"

"If you get a tattoo, you will go to hell!"

"We will all go to Heaven; there is no such thing as Hell!"

"The earth will be destroyed in 1472!"

"The earth will be destroyed in 2666!"

"God told me to kill my children!"

"Are you really saved? If you did not have a complete transformation when you accepted Jesus as Lord then you are not really saved."

"You are the biological daughter of God. You were created to be sacrificed to Him, so that His wrath will pass from us!"

"You are the descendant of Jesus and Mary Magdalene."

"Your deceased father wants you to know that he forgives you."

"Your deceased grandmother wants to tell you that she is watching over you and loves you very much."

The voices were loud. Some were shouting as if they were trying to be heard on a street corner, while others were calm and professional as if they were hosting a television program. I didn't understand what I was hearing. Some of the things said were lies, or perhaps they were all lies. Maybe that is why these words, their voices, the people were trapped here. They spewed lies.

The confusion of voices stopped and silence fell to the cave for a moment before they all erupted in unison:

"We are not false prophets! We speak truth! We called out to You, Lord, Lord. We speak truth! We did miracles in Your name. We speak truth!"

Wow! Even now, even when judgement had been passed and their crime had been found out, they still proclaimed a lie. I had heard about false prophets and psychics. I did not pay much attention, but I do remember one thing: false prophets and psychics acquire their information from Satan, whether they want to believe it or not, and true prophets of God get their information from God alone. Honestly, I thought all of them were jokes, people just trying to manipulate me, make a few bucks, or cause me to fear. I didn't fear and they never got a dime from me.

The eruption of lies began again, and the surrounding structure felt more unstable than it had when I first began to walk through the voices.

"I am the reincarnation of Moses! I will lead my people to freedom!"

"Go, drink this enchanted water and it will heal you."

"You will fall into great financial blessing tomorrow!"

"Your lucky numbers are seven, three, and two!"

"Tell the first three people you see that God loves them and you will be blessed all day!"

The passage of voices seemed to go on longer than I had walked thus far. It did end and the voices did begin to fade until I could no longer hear their proclamations of lies. Even though the voices had stopped, my ears seemed to have captured their echoes, and the pounding of their cries penetrated my thoughts and I could still hear them.

They believed their own lies. There was no conviction in their voices. Each one had probably led at least one person away from the truth. They brought those who listened and believed down this dark path, too. How dare they! I was proud that I had never fallen for their traps and deceit.

I had never fallen for their lies, however, had I fallen for the truth? What is the truth? God, surely I knew the truth.

I began to weep … or maybe I realized that I had been weeping all along, for I cannot remember a moment that tears did not fill my eyes or stream down my cheeks. "I want to live!

Forgive me! Bring me to life so that I can have a second chance!" I pleaded.

I closed my eyes, and expected to open my eyes and be standing in my home, or at least, somewhere I knew. When I opened my eyes, the darkness had not vanished. I must not be dead. I'm just trapped here with death. God would have answered that prayer. I was sincere. I would change. I said I would change given a second chance. I don't know what needs changing, but I would change. I will be more diligent in reading my Bible.

"God, if you get me out of here, I will give my house and car to the poor." I pleaded more, but with no result, no result I wanted anyway.

Isn't God a God of second chances? Why won't He give me a second chance?

"God, get me out of here!"

Why won't He listen? I've offered God everything and He won't take it. He is foolish! He can't exist! He doesn't exist! If God does exist, He must be in the far reaches of the universe and has nothing to do with us. Why would He create us only to leave us alone? Parents don't leave their children until the children are ready. Were we ready to be left to do our own bidding? The world could use a good parent to guide it. There is far too much hate, violence, injustice, pure wickedness for us to be left to walk the road alone. Because of the hate, violence and injustice, it proves that God is not a part of our lives. Doesn't it?

Why am I here? I'm not wicked. I never hurt anyone, not intentionally, not in my own knowing. I don't deserve this! I'm not guilty! Not guilty of anything!

Where am I going besides insane?

I turned my head to the side to look at the wall, to look where I had been trapped. I saw the shadows of the monsters almost beside me. It shocked me because I had almost forgotten that they had been following me.

"Go away!" I shouted. "Harass someone else! Just leave me alone!"

I watched the shadows completely ignore me and draw even closer. Their mouths opened and I could feel the warmth of their breath on my face. I could even hear a faint growl. Yet it wasn't until I could see their shadows begin to protrude from the wall that I dashed down the steps to get away from them. When I looked back and could no longer see the shadows, then and only then did I stop running. I didn't stop my descent. I merely slowed the pace.

The desire to be anywhere but here overcame me again, and I began to try to focus on food and drink. I needed food and water.

# 21

## Dining

I torture myself just as much as this tunnel of freak shows. The walls began to dissolve around me and the floor and ceiling became a real linoleum floor and plaster ceiling. A plastic table awaited me and a plate of food complete with a giant foam cup of drink begged to be consumed by me.

I sat down. The aroma flooded my nose, and could my mouth water, it would have. I reached for the food and found that I could not. Both of my hands were missing and part of my arms up to my elbows. I leaned forward and tried to remove the plastic cover over my food with my chin and mouth. Over and over I struggled with the container of food. Finally, like a dog, I took hold of the container with my mouth and shook violently until I could feel the lid give way. Food had oozed out through the seal of the lid and container and the gravy substance tasted of sulphur enriched vomit. With great difficulty, I managed to loosen the lid the rest of the way and tried to eat. I was so hungry, but the food made the hunger worse and I could not stomach the substance. It had smelled so good with the lid closed over it and now the fragrance of rotting waste turned my head from the one meal I had seen in days, weeks, months, possibly years. I would find no satisfaction in consuming it.

I turned toward the drink. Perhaps it would be better. There was no straw, but at least the lid was easier to deal with. In a few minutes, I had the lid off of the cup. With my lips on the rim, I tipped the cup toward my mouth and allowed the beverage to seep into my mouth. The flavor of urine and gasoline forced me to spit the beverage out immediately.

"How dare you serve this garbage!" I shouted.

My stomach began to churn, because it was empty or because it was upset by the vile food, I will never know. All I wanted to do was find a restroom to relieve myself in.

When I looked down, I was sitting on a toilet. Without hesitation, I went.

Even while I sat, the walls faded away and the floor returned to dirt. The ceiling trapped in the darkness. I stood, soiled, smelling as disgusting as the food I had tried to consume.

I detested my circumstance. I hated everyone, even the innocent were guilty for allowing me to go through this. God became abominable to me. His name became a curse. When I get out of here, I am going to kill everyone. No one will be safe. No one deserves to live. I hate all of you.

What am I talking about? Am I a murderer now? I guess I am. I cannot control the rage burning in my mind. I am hate. I am murder. I steal lives without a blink. What is this place that causes me to become evil? Not merely to experience the emotion of rage, but to become it. You probably cannot fathom what it is to become an emotion, to go beyond feeling. You probably think I'm mad, some sort of psychopath, and possibly I am. Just possibly, I am in a mental institute being treated for schizophrenia, psychopathic tendencies. Possibly I am insane and just don't remember going insane or ever being insane. Or just possibly, I am where I think I am, where I am beginning to accept that I am, either way, only one of us can be right. Do you want to take the chance that it is you?

# 22

# Revelation

Imagine a place void of comfort, peace, rest, joy, love, hope, mercy, compassion, life and all things righteous and good, and that is where I am at. I am in the embodiment of rage, pain, fear, selfishness, death and all things evil.

Shocked! Alone! Chaos! I wanted to die. Death will free me.

Why is God doing this to me? My life was so much easier before now. I didn't face anything painful.

"God, I must be alive. You wouldn't let anyone go through what I am going through without a way out. You are not that kind of God are you? If my only way out is death, then bring it!" I stopped on an unusually deep step. Most of the steps had been hardly as long as my foot. I began to spin around in a circle, and with my face toward the ceiling, I began to yell. Then I stopped spinning and began to stomp in a circle, jumping to make my point even clearer, though I'm not convinced that I really had a point apart from throwing the biggest temper tantrum in my life. Finally, I stopped and continued down, remembering that the beasts could catch up quickly.

I continued to plead, quite persistently, "Let me die! I want to die! God, take me to Heaven! I can't handle this insanity." Somehow the tears continued.

# 23

## Logic

The burning in my feet drew my attention away from my begging to die. I looked down and my shoes had been melted. Suddenly sanity came back to me, or maybe insanity was taking over again. I cannot distinguish one from the other. Either way, my mind for a moment seemed to clear and I was able to focus. At least, I think I was focused.

I rewrote my explanations for everything that I had been experiencing and ultimately deduced that the true reality of everything was that with each step I was heading deeper into a volcano. Why this explanation? It makes the most logical sense. This explanation touched the physical, tangible reality I was experiencing. This took into account everything that I felt and saw—the cave walls, the warmth of the air, the ever increasing heat. Everything else, my hallucinations, could also be explained as the result of heat exhaustion.

I knew … I really knew … beyond a shadow of a doubt that I was heading toward the center of a volcano. Lava had to be just below the surface to make the ground hot enough to melt my shoes.

I didn't want to move on. Who would? My hallucinations were growing weirder, more evil and more painful at every step. They were hallucinations; I demanded myself to accept this. And yet, I still wasn't convinced that I had not seen what I had, that I had not experienced what I had. All of it is so real. The people, or once people, each seem so real, so tangible. I could smell them. I could hear them. I could still hear them. The suffering screams and moans were echoing in my ears.

The pain does not go away. It increases; it pulsates; it thrives. My mind cannot make the pain go away; not like it has been able to manipulate my surroundings. I might suddenly find myself in a padded room, or a beach, or a hospital, or even my bedroom, but the pain … that pain is always present. It has to be a volcano. The heat is burning me; I can clearly see the evidence. The soles of my shoes are like chewing gum. My feet are blistered and rubbed raw and bleeding.

Even with this clearly logical revelation, there are still questions that I cannot answer. How did I get here? Why can I not ascend? Why do I keep heading deeper? Why am I so afraid of the walls? Do these unanswered questions negate my new revelation of what is happening to me? Am I or am I not heading to the heart of a volcano?

As much as I try to believe that I am heading to the mouth of a volcano, the truth of what is at the bottom of these spiraling steps is much worse than mere lava. The idea of lava toys with my nerves, and yet I will learn that lava is nothing, the fear of lava is absurd, the truth … the truth … no, I'm not ready for truth. Neither are many of you.

You read my tale, believing that it is some concocted story

to scare you. Perhaps you are right, but just perhaps, you are wrong. You read the ugliness, the pain, the emotions. You try to envision it. You wonder where this is going, if it will go anywhere. You deduce that it is a story and cannot be real. You tell me what is real? I will tell you, how dare you tell me that this isn't real, that this pain is made up! You cannot fathom it, so you believe this doesn't exist. It exists, and you might be stuck experiencing it firsthand if you don't find out the way to avoid it all together.

I cannot stop the growing fear. Hope is out of reach and no longer exists for me. Are we even able to extinguish all hope? Does a volcano warrant such hopelessness? Certainly not! The mystery, the unknown, that could easily warrant hopelessness, especially since there does not seem to be any reason to hope.

Am I giving my mind more credit than it is due? I have been saying that my mind is torturing me, that my mind has created these realities. Though it may seem I have been able to manipulate reality, changing the environment around me by mere wishful thinking, has it really changed and is it really me? The environment has upon multiple occasions changed in appearance, but the evil is still there, the hate is still there, and the pain is still there.

Doubt has once again gained control. My volcano theory explains some but not all. I wanted it to explain all. I needed it to explain all.

Here my thoughts are not my own. Deception lies at every bend. Am I deceiving myself or is someone else manipulating me? God, what is real? Why won't He answer me? Why am I walking this alone? God certainly isn't here. No one is here. I don't want to be alone, abandoned, not cared for, not loved, despised, hated, ignored, tossed out like garbage. I felt rejected. I felt that I wasn't good enough, not worth anyone's time.

I was angry at God. Didn't the Bible say that He would not

leave us? Well, He certainly broke His promise. I had never prayed as much or called on God as much as I was now.

The problem was that I didn't feel as though I deserved Him to answer. Why should He answer if I did not feel worthy? I felt condemnation for every little thing I had done or failed to do in my past. My past haunted me. I might have done many wonderful and good and at times righteous things, but the failures, the lies, the unforgiveness, the deceit, the pranks, the cheating, all of it ate away at my shriveled spirit.

Even those things that I had not done physically but was a momentary thought or desire made me feel like I had done the acts themselves. If I had merely wished someone dead, I felt like a murderer. If I had looked lustfully at a man, I felt like a fornicator. A little white lie felt like I had lied against God.

I did not deserve God, but I needed His help. The pain was too great! The chaos complicated my logic and thoughts. He would help. He was God. I was told that God always heard your cries for help.

"God, why are You silent? Don't abandon me now! I need You! I never needed You, not like now." I pleaded and begged for God to hear me, to answer me. Nothing. "Why am I walking this alone? Why are You ignoring me? What did I do to bring this wrath upon me? Aren't You real? Answer me!"

I was able to command more tears from my eyes. They rushed down my face; my cheeks burned from the salt. The abandonment hurt. My heart shattered. To feel so unloved, so rejected, so ignored. I felt invisible to God. I felt as though I never existed in His eyes. How could God do that? I went to church every Sunday, at least the Sundays that were convenient, which were most Sundays. I was faithful to go to church, so why is He not faithful now?

I don't want to be alone.

# 24

# Exhaustion

I wanted to stop. I needed to rest. I could clearly remember sleep, how wonderful a bed felt and the pillow beneath my head, how it felt to wake in the morning after a full night's sleep. It was something beautiful, something I took advantage of and never really thought to truly appreciate.

The last time I had wanted my bed, my sheets had tried to suffocate me. Now the idea of my bed brings me grief. I cannot have what I once had. It is no longer my right to have such comforts. Peace and rest is not something I can acquire. It is as far from me as the east is from the west.

My eyes cried to be closed and to remain so, but they felt glued open. When I did happen to succeed in closing my eyes, I would get sick to my stomach, and have to open them again immediately, which did not take away the uneasiness in my stomach but allowed me to focus on other discomforts.

My head pounded for rest. It would not stop. It would keep going, jumping from one thought to the next without finishing the first. This probably contributed to the inability to answer the questions that kept popping up. I would ask the question, and before I could logically or illogically come up with an explanation, I would be focused on my pain or on another question.

My body ached from the constant walking and sometimes running, always moving. Even when I paused, I could not find rest for my body. My body felt jittery from the exhaustion, shaking constantly. Every movement took great effort but I was not allowed to stop. With the shadow monsters behind me and some unseen force drawing me onward, I had to keep moving.

Have you ever gone a long time without sleep? How long? A day, a few days, a week, a month? After a long time of no sleep, your mind begins to make up stuff around you. You become paranoid. You see things that are not there. Your world becomes warped. Your body is stressed from the exhaustion; you cannot function. You have a nervous breakdown, go crazy, and for some you die.

Try never sleeping again, and you don't die. Shall I repeat myself? You do not die! You cannot rest. You cannot sleep. And you do not die! You live, or at least, you continue. Your body trembles, shakes, sways, and yet, you will not collapse from fatigue. The paranoia, the hallucinations, all physical breakdown rewrites your DNA and you become madness, and you cannot stop it. You are not permitted, not privileged to rest.

I just wanted to sleep. I would take five minutes, any amount that would be offered just to rest. I would give up my right arm, both arms, just to sleep for five minutes.

Have you ever had to walk for a long distance? Competed in

a marathon? Had to move constantly for a great distance? How far? A few miles? A few hundred miles? After a while, your body feels the stress. With no nourishment to keep you going, you don't last long at all. Try walking around the earth, swimming across the oceans, climbing over the mountains without the aid of anyone or anything. Do this without food or water. You will die.

Here you don't die. You just continue. Your body weakens from the stress. Your joints grind against one another and are swollen to a point where you shouldn't even be able to move them, yet you manage it anyway. You are not given food or water, but you do not die. You suffer.

God, I would give You everything if I could just die.

# 25

# Suffering

I had witnessed far too much evil, too much pain. I was being sucked into this madness. I was beginning to believe and accept that this place is … No, I won't go there. I cannot. If I go there, then I know there is no way out. There has to be a way out. I had to figure out why I was insane and fix the problem. My bottom lip quivered, but I wasn't cold, I was terrified at all that I had seen and what I could possibly see next.

Nothing brought me comfort. Even those things that I felt could not possibly harm me: my bed, a beach, food, brought me more agony. My mind tormented me over and over. There was no peace, no ease, no relief.

The path began to brighten a little the farther I descended. One would think that it would get darker. But I could see a little clearer. I didn't want to see. What I saw … I didn't want to see.

The tunnel continued. It never ended. I have to be miles deep into the earth. There is a center isn't there? I should be coming up the other side. As long as I have walked, I know I have traveled thousands of miles.

As I have said, or will say, time does not exist. Fathom it the best you can, but understand it is no more. Here you just are. I have only recounted a fraction of what I have gone through, what I am going through and what I will go through. I have been here forever, even though I do remember my time before forever. You think I do not make sense, that I am contradicting myself, perhaps I am and yet it is as I say it is.

I have traveled thousands upon thousands of miles and can find no end!

Where are all the diamonds and gems that are supposed to be here deep in the earth? Shouldn't there be diamonds the size of my head or larger? There is nothing of the like. There are skeletons, human skeletons and only human skeletons. No animal, no dinosaur bones.

Science has it all wrong. God created science. If so called scientists would not keep trying to use what God created to prove that God does not exist, then possibly all of this would make more sense. We would have fewer theories and more truths. God, I believe in You! Why did You let me come here?

My heart suddenly raced, and my breathing increased. My stomach felt as though I had swallowed a knife and it was tearing its way through my intestines. The pain pulsated, and each time there was a smidge of ease, the pain would increase. No scale is high enough to compare to the pain I felt. The walls swayed more than they had been, the ground turned to quicksand, and I worked hard, struggling with whatever I could muster, trying to stay above it and not give up and allow the floor to consume me.

I grabbed my stomach as if to comfort it, but without success. I wanted to vomit and faint at the same time. The overwhelming dread I felt for having to continue further smothered me with anxiety. I yanked one foot from within the ground and flung it forward. I then yanked the next foot out of the sinking sand. With a pop, the ground released me. I then swung my leg with such force that I tripped and stumbled forward.

I was going to hit the ground! I had made it past the quicksand, or that quicksand, for I will face more areas where the ground will actually succeed in swallowing me only to spit my crushed body out so that it can do it all over again later. I saw the ground approaching my face. My knees were inches from the insects that covered the ground.

# 26

## A Hospital Or Hell?

Desperate to catch my balance before I hit the ground, I flung my arms out. I was so desperate, that I was willing to touch the cave walls, the very walls I feared. Yet instead of touching a jagged rock wall, my fingers fell to a cold, smooth surface. I did not look at my hands or the surface of which they touched. I looked beyond them down the hall.

"The hospital!" I shouted. The white walls! The light! "Let me just stay here," I added.

Then I remembered the beast or at least the roaring from the previous visit. The anxiety rose within me. The memory of the event became more real than when I had experienced it. I struggled to hear the roar this time, preparing my emotions and my body for the worst. There was nothing, only the soft humming of the air conditioning. What if the beast comes back? But then I realized, I didn't care. The beast could not compare to what I just experienced. My stomach was almost back to normal.

I stood and turned around to look down the other end of the hall. I felt a quick disorientation. After shaking the fog from my eyes and mind and very much to my surprise, I was no longer standing. I was flat on my back, and I was not in the hallway anymore, but in a patient's room. My hands gripped the side rails of a hospital bed. This time, no one was over me. An IV tube was attached to one hand and my other arm was attached to a blood pressure and heart rate monitor. These and these alone kept me in the bed, nothing else restrained me. I could easily remove the tubes and leave the bed. Yes … yes, my legs had sensation. I could get up out of the bed if I wanted to.

According to the monitor, I had a steady pulse and blood pressure. I was in fine shape, so why was I in a hospital? It wasn't for physical reasons.

Resting back on the pillow, I looked up at the ceiling. The florescent lighting burned my eyes, producing a headache beginning from behind my eyes and moving up toward my temples. I had been in the darkness for too long this last time. I didn't want to rest my eyes for fear of returning to the cave. This reality worked for me. I would prefer to remain here, even if I was alone, even if there was a beast.

I still had not heard the roar and finally took a well-deserved sigh of relief. For the first time in who knows how long, I felt hope. Here I had hope, real hope. Hope that everything would turn out okay and that I would not go back to that dark place.

Here, I accepted that I was insane, embraced it with open arms. I accepted that I was in a hospital. I accepted that here I could acquire the help I needed. The doctors could help me. God did not allow the torment here. I just needed to stay here. In the cave, spiraling down the tunnel, there was no hope, no help, and I could not get better. I could only dwell on the negative, the oppression, and most certainly the depression and fear. Here, oh, I just wanted to stay here. Here, I didn't want to die. However, I was alone. But does it matter? I'm not in pain. I don't feel anything. I am numb, emotionally, mentally, and spiritually numb. There is numbness. I can live with numbness. I was even beginning to forget the cave. Forget what I had seen. Forget what I might still see. Forget that I always seemed to go back to the darkness, to the tunnel, to the trap. Let me stay here. Please, God, let me stay here.

A creaking noise in the room brought my attention to another patient beside me. I wasn't alone after all. An elderly woman was sitting up in the hospital bed next to me, crossing her arms and rocking back and forth. Company, a possible friend, and yet I could sense an emptiness in her, a deception, an ugliness. Was she real? She did not look at me. Her focus was on the wall across from us. Her gown was dingy, and I felt sorry for her. I felt compassion for someone other than me. It was a welcomed feeling. I wanted to talk to her, but was distracted by the feeling of heat at the foot of the bed. I looked down at my feet . . .

# 27

## Help!

I caught myself before I could hit the ground. The tunnel had narrowed; the walls were close enough that I could reach out and touch both with either hand. I had grabbed the walls! My hands slid down the sediment while I tried to brace myself. I straightened back up, but not before I realized that sharp fragments from the tunnel walls had sliced at my palms. In an awkward delayed reaction, I screamed in pain. Removing my hands quickly after balancing myself, I looked and saw that several bone chips had lodged in my hands like broken glass. I picked them out of my flesh and dropped the pieces to the floor. I wiped my bloody palms on my shirt and then continued my descent. What will happen once I get to the bottom?

I protected my hands by cupping them to my lower chest. I almost looked like I was praying, though I was far from it at the moment. I had moved past prayer and went straight to begging. Begging must be beneath God. He did not answer that either. Am I so despicable that not even begging moves God to action? Scum. I am complete scum.

Why was my mind trapped in the cave? Why was I alone? Why weren't there answers? I know I have repeated these questions over and over, but until I have an answer, and an acceptable one, I will continue to ask.

There was a silence around the next curve that almost made me wish I could hear the moaning again. In a side cavern, as large as several football stadiums, there were over a million children of all ages in this space. You mock and ask if I counted. Do you not remember me saying that here you just know things? I knew there were more than a million children, children of all ages, size, gender, race, and ethnicity.

Some of the children were transfixed on a blank television screen. They could not tear their eyes from the empty screen. I could see that all of them wanted to look elsewhere, even close their eyes, but the link between them and the screen was too strong. I could see the struggle, the tears falling down their cheeks, the veins in the face and neck burst in their fight against the invisible pull.

Others were literally attached to gaming controllers – controllers were fused to their hands, sticking out from their heads or chests, cords wrapped around their necks. One child had controllers instead of hands. This child tried to pull the controllers off, but could not. Every time, the pain would be too great, and blood would gush from the buttons, and the child would cry and stop, only to try again a few seconds later, an evil repetitious cycle.

A group of children sat at a huge dining table, bare of food. These children acted as if they were starving, desperate for any kind of food. They tore at the fat from their own stomachs and munched on it. They were eating their own flesh! They chewed like starved wild animals, viciously and without reproach.

Still others were filled with so much anger, they threw punches and kicks at the other children. They were unsuccessful in their attacks however, and every punch, bite, or kick, sent them whirling into a jutting wall face. These children were battered beyond recognition. Their arms and legs were broken, their faces bashed in, ribs stuck out from their chest or back, brain matter hung from open wounds in their skulls, and yet they continued to try to fight and were continuously bashed against the wall by an invisible force.

Some children were attached to a creature, a demon-like creature. This creature for some was like a second head with a second neck that protruded from their shoulder, like a Siamese twin. For others, the demon creature protruded from their chest and shared a heart, while others had a creature wrapped around their waist, or arm or leg.

Each demon looked different – some had scales, others fur, several had feathers, or a combination. There were many that had a skin texture that was completely unknown to me. The demons were dark, gray in color and were transparent. They hissed, growled, or roared at the scared children. They bit, choked, or scratched the children, harassing and abusing them most violently.

These children all bore a mark, the same mark across their forehead, the mark of sin and death.

They had been dedicated to other gods, to demons, to Satan. Upon dedication, a demon was attached to each child. This demon was bound to this child forever.

How could anyone do this to their own child? These children

suffered the most, as their demon continuously tormented and taunted them. They could not escape the demon. They could never escape their tormentor. I heard their cries of curses on their parents. I would have been glad that I was not their parent could I have felt gladness. I knew that most of their parents were down here, too. Their bodies made up part of the walls of the cavern the children were in and their ears were forced to hear the agony of the children for eternity.

I looked away, knowing that had I been given a choice to dedicate my child to Satan to free me from this place I would. Don't you dare turn your nose against me! If you were here, you would do the same thing or worse.

There were other fixations, obsessions going on with other children, but I could not bear to look on any more than I already had. I wanted to burn the images from my mind, and I probably could have if I rested my head on the volcanic floor. At one point in my life I would have wanted to cry for the children, but now, like everyone else I had come across, I didn't care. Selfishness was my reward. Besides, I realized that those children had given their souls to those things that now completely possessed them: television, gaming, food, books, sports, music, hate, sex, violence…

Suddenly the shadow monsters leapt into the cavern and attacked the children. Some of the children pushed other children into the path of the monsters, trying to escape, only to be snatched up by a monster later. Limbs were being torn off, and what the smaller demons failed to do, the monsters were successful in doing.

Many of the children wanted to cry for their parents. They were desperate to be comforted. I could sense what they were going through and my heart shattered again. But the broken heart was not for them. I felt the pain for me. Their pain had become my pain. I had to get away from them. They would have to get their comfort from someone or something else.

Wandering around in the blackness with an orange glow that offered enough light to let me know that I was still trapped, my psychological steadiness was rocky at best. No pun intended, in fact, to me, my own wording seemed in poor taste. By now, a steady stream of self-pitying tears remained constantly stamped across my face. The ends of my hair and my shirt neck were drenched with the salty liquid.

Facing the agony, feeling the relentless pain, I began to accept ... no ... I knew that whatever this place was, wherever this place was, it was real. This cannot be something my mind merely made up. My imagination had been good, but never would I have created this in my thoughts. It was too evil, too painful, too real.

I began to hate even my most dearly beloved for leaving me in this place, for not coming to my rescue. I would have most certainly come for them. At least, I would have tried. My mind toyed with ideas of how to get back at them for this evil, that is, if I ever find my way out of this Godforsaken place. I could lock them up in a basement for a year, giving them only vinegar to drink and raw meat to eat. Or, I could also trap them in a cave, sealing the entrance. Or, I could just toss them into a giant oven and turn up the heat.

It is so hot!

I hated even myself for allowing this to happen to me. How did I let my guard down? Why did I let my guard down? Why? I don't understand. I am always so careful. How did this happen? Where are my family, my friends, all those of whom I've helped and supported over the years? Why did they leave me here? Why have they abandoned me? How could they leave me here alone? Are they even looking for me? What did I do to deserve this? I was a good person; I am a good person. Won't someone have pity on me? Won't someone help me?

Where is God?

As I continued on, the silence was broken by the screams of the cave. The cries of the children were not for my ears, so I had not heard them. Even those that I said I had heard spewing curses upon their parents, I had not heard with my ears but it was more of a telepathic connection – I heard them in my mind; I understood them without the oral confirmation. My mind pulsated with their cries, but my ears had not been affected.

Ahead of me … always ahead of me … more torment awaited. You think that the worst thing I've seen by far is the children. Yes, the children are sad, but it is not the worse thing down here. You don't want to believe that children are here, but they are. You would like to believe that all children are innocent, but they are not. Do you not remember your childhood? Hiding from your authority the things you knew in your heart were not good to do. You were guilty even then.

My hands still hurt and will always hurt, so I continued to protect them, though it will not be long before I accept that trying to protect them is fruitless. The cuts will never heal. For the moment however, I protected them, holding them against my chest.

I carefully took the steps, moving unnaturally slow. My balance was off since I did not have my arms free and I did not want to slip again. Not far from the cavern of children did I come upon something blocking my descent.

# 28

## God?

A creature groveled in front of me. A tattered, white garment held on to the boney flesh and splotches of blood kept it in place. Its dark hair clung to its face, wet from I don't know what. I half wanted to suck the moisture from its hair. I was so thirsty. I could see the shadows of the eye sockets through slivers of parts in the hair, but I could not see the eyes themselves. What was I looking at?

My eyes were the unkindest parts of my body. Even my nerves, which introduced me to new pains at every turn, did not compete with my eyes which tormented me with new horrendous visions every chance they got, visions that would not go away. The visions remained constant in my sight. Even long after the object was gone, the image echoed, never ending, imprinting itself to my thoughts.

"Who are you?" I asked after trying to pass it and failed.

It had countered my move and blocked my path. If I could have gotten past it, I would have. Finally, I looked at it. Really looked at it and saw that for the most part, this person was intact which gave me counterfeit hope. Hope that I was not alone; hope that I had been found; hope that I could escape. I knew it wasn't hope even then, but I still chose to hold onto whatever it was. For a moment, I ignored that the hope was false, but the reality of it being false would show itself soon enough.

The creature did not respond. Could this creature help me? Better yet, would this creature help me? So far I was unsuccessful in finding anyone who could help. Not even God would tell me how to get out of here.

"I'm trying to find my way out of here. Can you help me? Will you lead the way?" I waited what seemed like seconds and hours all at once before the person acknowledged that I was there.

Looking right into my eyes, the person stepped closer and I could smell spoiled fish emitting from it. A raspy voice emitted from black lips. "Are you a god?" it asked me.

That one insane question tore the counterfeit hope from my chest, laughed at it and stomped it into the ground. A god?! I don't know why I kept allowing hope or whatever it is to manifest itself in my heart and mind! It was knocked down, bashed in, stepped on over and over. I was knocked down, bashed in, and stomped on. It wasn't even an act of humbling me; it was an act of humiliating me.

Was it even hope that I was feeling? I don't remember what hope feels like.

I was pleading for change, for anywhere, for anything but here, but this. This can't be it for me, not here.

"God, why am I being shown all of this? Why am I going through all of this?" I asked aloud and paused and waited. Not really expecting a response, but giving Him an opportunity anyway. "What are You trying to teach me?"

The person in front of me didn't hear a word I said. In fact, it was as though my entire conversation with God had never happened. I refocused my attention—for what it was— back on the person before me and what it had said.

A god?! Who asks that? Of course, I'm not a god! Would a god allow himself or herself to be trapped here? Did this creature not hear me? I was trying to find a way out. Would a god ask for help? This stupid imbecile! This idiot! I'm an idiot, too, for thinking that this person, or anyone who is also stuck down here, would show me a way out. If anyone knew the way out, they would no longer be here. They would be an even bigger asinine creature than all of us combined for remaining in a place like this if they were able to escape and did not.

I was exhausted. My emotions were spent. My sanity, my grip on reality, was lost forever. I had no fight in me. Wasn't God supposed to fight my battles anyway? I've been doing all the fighting. All my life I fought, able to do it myself, and now when I need Him, He abandons me.

My emotions shut down momentarily. I locked away fear, shock, pity, confusion, even agony. My companion now was apathy. Monotone and with no source of emotion, I replied, "No, I'm not a god." I wanted to end this conversation and continue down the steps. I didn't want anything to do with this person. I had nothing more to say. I almost wanted to push it out of the way, but that would have displayed emotion and as I have said, for the moment, my emotions were shut off. I could not access them if I wanted to. This could have been a result of shock, but I was beyond shock, for the moment even shock was an emotion. I was a block of stone: lifeless, heartless, faithless. Nothing could move me.

The creature ignored me so I tried to go around it again. It blocked my way again. "I'm a fervent follower to my religion," it interrupted. "I worshiped and served my gods relentlessly. Due to my obedience and pureness, I was selected to be a sacrifice for my people. I was pleased and honored to take on such a role."

The idea of human sacrifice revived my humanity, or what one can consider as humanity here. Most people agree that human sacrifice is barbaric. I always thought that it was barbaric, horrific, inhuman. How could anyone justify wasting a human life, and for what purpose, to satisfy some inanimate object, an object manmade that offers no more power than the element in which it is made out of? Or worse, sacrificing to a man or an animal that has no more power than the strength of its body, and no more wisdom than its own understanding.

I had thought that human sacrifice had been abolished, outlawed, was of ancient times. But here I was face to face with a human offering, and worse yet, a human offering that wanted to be sacrificed, that had been honored to be sacrificed. It was all in vain. What good did it do? This person is here. Was it supposed to go to some kind of heaven? Because this isn't any kind of heaven of any people I ever heard about, and if it is, then why in the world would they want to come here. Not even Hell can be worse than this.

I was face to face with someone who had been used as a sacrifice to appease the people's superstitions. I accepted this as complete fact. Why accept it as anything else? No one could come up with a story equal to this. This person had been alive and is now dead because its tribe or whatever felt it necessary to end its life to satisfy their false gods.

I have been facing death over and over. God, is there no life here? Is this my reward for all the good I did? Why must I face this – more and more death, death at every bend?

114

This burnt offering before me was nuts. Why would anyone sacrifice themselves to a bunch of gods? Didn't it know that there is only one God? And that we don't sacrifice ourselves to Him? Perhaps that is the point, we don't sacrifice ourselves to Him, yielding our lives to Him. Perhaps we merely add God to our lives instead of surrendering our lives to God. If I had yielded my life to God, would I be here? I yield it now! I surrender it now!

I paused again, and this time I waited a little longer. Nothing. Is it too late? Maybe God didn't hear me. I'll remind Him again later. I surrender myself to Him. I'm not really sure what that means or what it entails, but I do it anyway.

Did this person not realize that sacrificing itself to false gods was fruitless? I don't believe it did. Not even now, after the sacrifice had come and gone did this pathetic person accept that it had been denied. It had been rejected, considered unworthy. Its life had been treated like a pile of trash and had been tossed out as such.

It continued talking!

"My people carried me down to the water's edge and bound me to a stone. When the god of the sea came to receive me, the waters rushed upon me. I guess I was not worthy of the god. My life was pointless. Not one of my gods came to take me away. I asked myself if they even existed, then I repented for doubting them. I sacrificed myself again on an altar I built in there." A finger pointed toward a cavern that had not been there a moment before.

My heart broke again. Is that how God saw me, how my family and friends saw me, as pointless? My life isn't pointless. I almost felt as though it had directed that statement directly to me. "No life is pointless!" I argued, yet I almost doubted my own words. From what I had already witnessed, perhaps some lives were pointless, though maybe it has to do with how one uses his life while he has it. My life wasn't pointless. My life isn't pointless. I'm still alive. I shouldn't be here! This is all a test. I figured it out. This is a test. God is testing me, but what for? I always helped people.

I looked into the cavern and saw a bolder in the center of the room and I presumed the bolder acted as an altar. The cavern reeked of death, burnt flesh. I succumbed to the idea of being burned alive or drowned. My physical pain seemed to mimic what I had imagined the person had felt when it first was drowned and then when it decided to burn itself just to be sure it had indeed been sacrificed. I toppled over in anguish, though I did not fall completely to the ground nor rest on the walls. I fought the force that pushed me to fall the rest of the way or to fall upon the wall, and I hung in the air crouched in an almost fetal position, as I could feel the flames lapping at my arms and legs and torso and my lungs and throat gurgle with unquenchable water.

Pointing the same finger in my face, "That is where you are wrong!" it said in response to my comment that no life is pointless, and I was freed from the force and stood. I could feel my own pain and did not like that I was forced to feel others' pain as well. I began to agree that its life was most assuredly pointless. "And for wasting my life on gods who have no power and no immortality, my eternal resting place, my eternal damnation is here in this pit of fire, where all of my mortal pleasures only cause me more pain. I hope your past life was kind to you because this death that you are now a part of is far from pleasant." It concluded.

Dead? The only thing that is dead is my sense of humor. If I were dead, I'd be in Heaven, not Hell. I was a good person. I spent my life volunteering, helping others, giving. God wouldn't send me here.

Uneasily, I looked around at the narrow path with eyes that

were open to the idea that I might be dead. The rocks moved again. There were things crawling all over the walls. Insects covered the walls and the floor. They crawled onto my exposed feet and ate away at the skin, tissue, and through the muscle to the bone. I could see my bones and I was still alive, still conscious. I stomped around, but the insects remained in place, unaffected by my efforts.

The sacrifice disrupted my wondering mind by walking into the cavern. I stepped to the opening and took a closer look at the altar. The scratches in it looked to have been carved by fingers. It crawled on top of the stone and kneeled, "Oh great spirits of the earth, sea and sky, I come before you to offer up a gift. Please accept me as a sacrifice to you." It proceeded to lie down on the slab. The little girl who keeps popping up right then materialized in the cave. Quickly she stabbed the knife into the human sacrifice's chest, and then just as quickly she pulled it out. A flame then came up from the altar and consumed the person who had lain upon it. Horrified, I stepped away. I tried to take in a breath, but the air would not enter. I turned and staggered down the steps trying to get away from the madness and the murderous child.

Steps away from the sacrifice, another cavern revealed yet another heinous act. A skeletal being with one hand and the entire digestive track intact, commenced ripping away the flesh off a human leg with its teeth. It chewed and swallowed the meat. My stomach churned at the sight. I kept walking, and the noise around me echoed in loud chatter. Shrill screams, singing, moaning, laughter, crying, all bounced off the stone walls and vibrated through my ears. My head throbbed. I walked on.

Upon the next bend . . .

# 29

# Why Am I Here?

Blinking to readjust my eyesight to the brightness, I was aware that I was back in the hospital without having to see anything. I could smell the disinfectants and feel the effects of the high concentration of oxygen in the air. I was flat on my back and cold. I was back in the patient's room. Why did I keep coming back here?

I've noticed that the hospital is the only place I keep coming back to now. Then again, I haven't really tried to conjure up anywhere else in my mind since the last mishap. How does the saying go: 'fool me once shame on you, fool me twice shame on me?' Well, I fooled and shamed myself more than twice, so I gave up. Not so … I just got to a point where I could not think of anywhere that would be safe to think of. I had thought of all the most peaceful places I knew and each place proved fatal. I could no longer think of a safe place. My mind went completely blank on this subject. So I cannot fathom why I kept coming back to the hospital. I never thought about the hospital. I just simply kept popping up here with no warning and no justification, at least, no justification I could understand.

Remembering the old woman from last time, I was about to turn my head to look at her, when I realized that my head would not turn. I was paralyzed all over, unable to move even a finger. I could move my eyes, however, the position of my head still prevented me from seeing if the old woman was still in the neighboring bed.

I heard a deep voice, which distracted all other thoughts. Continuing to lie on the bed, eyes wide open, I directed my gaze down toward the foot of the bed without moving my head. A doctor was standing there talking with another man who sat on the edge of the bed. The man was my husband!

I don't know why, but I called him darling, even though I sincerely hated my husband for allowing me to be trapped in the cave. "Darling, what's wrong?" I asked, and though I could hear the question in my mind, my voice was not heard by my ears. With the lack of response by the two men who spoke over me, I concluded that they had not heard me either. In fact, I don't think my lips had even mouthed the question.

"She has lost a lot of blood," the doctor said.

For a second, I must have actually gotten through to them that I was conscious, because they both looked at me. There was not a single emotional flicker in either of their faces, which struck me as odd. It was as though neither of them cared that I was conscious. My husband had always been a compassionate man and now, he looked … hollow. They both gave off a hollowness, as if they were a reflection and not the real thing. They did not even look real, as if they were plastic.

They seemed to note that I was awake and mumbled the rest of their conversation. I think they said the words 'ward' and 'under observation.' What did all that mean?

I closed my eyes. I was so tired. I felt like I had been awake for days, and yet, how could that have been so? I had lost a lot of blood, that's what the doctor said. Maybe that's why in my delusions there were so many gruesome sights. Maybe I died and then I was brought back to life. That would explain why I'm visualizing death. 'Under observation' could mean that, I couldn't understand why, but maybe I tried to kill myself. No, I don't think that's right. Someone tried to hurt me, but who?

I couldn't stay awake. As much as I fought it, I just couldn't stay awake. I . . .

# 30

## Dead Or Alive?

Had I remained awake, would I have ended up back here? Something always distracted me, bringing me back here, whether it was the sensation of burning in my feet, or being unable to stay awake. I always ended up back here. One place or the other is real. I much preferred it be the hospital. I could see the enemy coming and prepare myself. Here, I saw nothing and the enemy was always all around me and in me.

Why am I here? I don't deserve this. This should not be my end reward. I don't belong here. Evil belongs here. I am not evil. This is not justice, not for me. I was good, I gave to the poor, I gave to my church, so why am I here? What did I do wrong? Who did I hurt to deserve this? Does anyone have an answer?

Do you have an answer?

I tried to remember more. I could not. What happened to me? The initial questions which I had asked at the beginning of this hell-plotted journey flooded back to me, and I began to ask them again. How did I get here? I finally knew who I was, at least my name. I had almost not recognized my own husband. Who am I? What is my past? What happened to me?

Am I drifting between life and death? God, I want to live! I don't want to be here. The pain is beyond what any one person should ever go through. The aloneness, I hate how alone I am. I don't merely feel alone. I know I am alone and will always be alone.

I soon realized that I was standing still, not moving like I knew I should constantly be doing. I glanced over my shoulder just in time to see a paw with sharp nails come down hard on my shoulder blade. Before the shadow monsters could attack again, I ran. The pain in my back, for the moment, hurt much worse than my hands, so I began to swing my arms to help balance me while I ran. I ran so hard and faster than I had ever run before in my life that I slowed and came to a steady walk after a minute of speed.

The abyss of my fears engulfed me. This was all a delusion. But, how could I turn this delusion off? With the physical pain so great, it became almost impossible to continue to believe that this place wasn't real, and yet, I just could not accept that it was. Still not grasping the truth that stood before me, still bewildered, still shocked, I continued my descent knowing that my answers lay at the bottom of the tunnel. Though at moments, I didn't believe there could be a bottom.

A song popped in my head. A song that I had been taught when I was a little girl in Sunday School. It was a song about the books of the Bible. Before I knew what I was doing, I was singing the lyrics, "Gen-e-sis, Ex-o-dus, Levit-icus, Numbers,

Deut-er-onomy." Those stupid words tortured me. They were the titles of books of the Bible, and yet, had I read them? Sure, even more than once. But had I embraced them? Did I leave the Bible having only read the words, or did I walk away knowing more of who God was, learning from the messages, allowing the words to change me? Did I believe the Bible was real, or did I merely hope it was? Was hoping enough?

"When I get out of here, I'm going to read my Bible and allow it to change me," I proclaimed aloud. For a moment, I almost believed myself – that I would get out … that I would read the Bible … that I would change.

An earthquake shook the cave. This vibration was much stronger than what the false prophets had managed to create. The earthquake did not bring any of the walls or ceiling crashing down on me, yet it caused the floor to open up before me. A monster, using long, sharp claws, dragged himself up from the hole created by the quake. The mud caked to his body most likely doubled his size.

"What are you screeching? The books of the Bible? How stupid and pathetic! They won't help you down here," he growled at me.

Offended, I countered, "They can't hurt!" The only person who can say such things to me is me! I had had enough of everything and everyone. Everyone was telling me what was what, well those who spoke did, and yet they said nothing at all. Their words were insignificant and completely pointless, helping in no way at all in answering my questions.

In frustrated contempt, I put my hands over my face and cried. The monster was right. The song did not help my situation, and in that moment, instead, it seemed to just make the matter worse.

"Stop your crying!" he roared. "Crying won't get you anywhere either!"

125

I rung my fingers through my hair and squeezed my own head in further frustration. I obediently stopped bawling, but the steady stream of tears continued to flow. I don't think the tears ever stopped. No, they have not. I've already told you that. You constantly cry here. You cannot help it. Even when I had accepted everything and had managed to lock up my heart for a minute, the stream of tears flowed. Every tear burned my skin.

I could see that my obedience to his commands pleased and pained him at the same time. I could see the torment and division in him. I even understood it. He was angry, probably even more than me. I feared what he might try to do, and worse, what he might succeed in doing to me.

My head felt new pain, and when I took my hands away from my head, clutched in both hands was a wad of hair. On top of everything, my hair was falling out! No, I had pulled my hair out, though it had come out easily. Looking up at him, I paid particular attention to the fact that he, too, was bald. For a split second, my mind wondered and I quickly surmised that I must be undergoing chemo treatments in the hospital. But that didn't make any sense. What's wrong with me?!

"What's wrong with me?" I screamed at the hair in my hands. I knew that the bald man would not answer me. My questions were not answered by anyone. They seemed to be unanswerable. They fell on deaf ears, on selfish ears, on no ears at all. Everyone had to be a concoction of my mind, and since I didn't know the answers, neither did they. Why would I torture myself like that? What happened to me that I would be sent here?

This man wore a uniform, military of some sort or another. I thought I recognized the antique garb, but I couldn't place it. His physical features were more recognizable than the Picasso, and yet, he looked melted. In one swift motion, he reached out and took hold of my throat. "Nothing will help you down here."

*Dead Or Alive?*

I pushed myself free from him, detaching one of his hands and knocking it to the floor. He bent over, picked it up, and shoved it back into his body in a place different from where it had been attached. I allowed my eyes to widen in incredulity.

I wanted to escape. From all the other creatures, or persons depending on your prospective, this particular one gave me room to move past him. The hole in the stairs had not completely gone all the way across the tunnel, so I slipped up to the wall and moved slowly down a couple of steps. I now stood right beside the middle of the hole. I froze from fear. If I continued, I risked slipping through the hole.

I glanced back at the uniformed man and noticed that he had come toward me, a look of rage in his face. In my desperation to get away, I did not take heed to my fear, and moving too quickly, I ended up stepping right into the hole. I fell through the floor and landed on my feet breaking more than one bone. With new pain, with more pain, I stumbled back and rammed my shoulder against a rock face. A sensation worse than my feet swallowed up my shoulder blade, the very shoulder blade the shadow monster had attacked.

I had touched the walls again! I twisted my head back to look at the spot, and further explored the area by feeling the spot when I stood erect. A bone lodged itself through the shoulder and into the blade. I couldn't pull it out myself. The military man jumped down, landing in front of me. I was still in the narrow, spiral staircase, just a couple of bends lower.

I had no wish to stay longer in his presence than I had to. I tried to get around him again. He had other plans for me. He grabbed my arms and held me there. In terror, I screamed and he slapped me. "I was a great leader. Power was mine and my people obeyed me, and so will you!" He pushed me to a sitting position on the steps. My legs and buttocks burned; they were on fire, but I could not move. "I ruled over a great nation. We

were ready to conquer the world. I only had to give the order."
I chose not to look at him, even though I could feel him smiling
down at me. "I ordered it. We were the superior race and I was
their leader. It was for the sake of all of humanity that we
restore order among chaos. We had to first rid ourselves of the
weaker races that would only taint the earth with their filth." He
bent over and looked into my horror-stricken face. "Yes, that's
right. You understand me, don't you? I ordered the total
inhalation of billions of people, all in the name of purifying the
earth."

I had to get away. "You're mad! You crazy old fool! Why
are you doing this to me?" I leaned forward to slide past him.
He countered the move and this time tossed me down several
steps. A crunching noise in my left leg ended my tumbling. The
crippling pain kept me from trying to escape.

"No, woman! You're mad!" He confirmed my own
suspicions. Being crazy was the only thing that made sense, and
yet, it didn't. I could think clearly, and wasn't it a fact, that if
you said you were crazy than you most likely weren't? He kept
talking, "You haven't even realized where you really are.
You're the one that's delusional. I know where I am. I knew
what my purpose was. I had my army mutilate men, women and
children. We were making a way for a new superior people to
occupy this pathetic earth. And you know what, I don't regret a
single order I gave. I don't regret a single death of a child. They
were all impure, not one innocent." He came toward me. I had
to touch the rock walls to pull myself up. The walls were no
longer rock, bone, or parts of human bodies; they were soft,
almost like magma. My hands burned, and I looked at them. The
skin had been seared off, and I could see down to the bones. He
delighted in my pain. "The only thing I regret is not succeeding,
and being stuck here with impure races all around me, unable to

escape them. Many of those that I had murdered come to me to haunt me now. I just haunt them back!"

"Why are you telling me this?" I screamed at him.

He leapt up through the hole and it closed behind him. Maybe this is some sick game. Maybe I was abducted by aliens and they have implanted some sick memories into my mind, or maybe this is some distorted virtual world, I've found myself in. Now, I do sound crazy. I'm tired of all the maybes. I want it all to end. "Let me die!"

# 31

## Fear

There is only so much you can say about fear. Everyone experiences fear at some point in their lives, granted, some more than others. For some, the extremity of the emotion is so great that it is diagnosed as a phobia, and in that, it also has different levels of severity.

I cannot believe that anyone has or ever could experience the terror I feel in this uncertain place. As I have said, I have become fear. My body is walking, talking, tangible fear. Every cell is fear. My genetic makeup has been rewritten with fear at its base. My mind takes me from a hospital to the very pit of hell. There is no one, not one creature to share my misery, to lighten my load, or to even offer a kind word. There are hideous monsters all around me and all they can do is magnify the lonesomeness I feel at the pit of my stomach and scare the life out of me.

I cannot feel my heart beat anymore: whether it races or slows remains a mystery to me, though I can sense the panic in my chest when I come around the next spiral and see that there is still rock, stairs, and no sign of an exit.

The questions that aren't answered, or the answers that I can't make sense of, all of it, just taints my mind with insanity. I want to cry, I do cry, but what purpose does it serve? I find no relief in shedding tears. My face is permanently stained with red streaks from the hot tears I already wept and still weep. My tear ducts are dry. I know they are dry; they burn from the dryness, and yet, moisture still pours down, the blood vessels have burst under the stress, and for a while my tears were mixed with blood, until it was only blood. Even now, I know my blood has, too, dried up and yet there are still tears. I cannot tell you what their liquid source is, but I constantly cry.

Fear and depression are inseparable. As I have become fear, I am also depression itself. Do you understand that? To not live with depression, to not merely feel depressed occasionally, but to become deep sadness. It is something you can never shake, never get away from, never get over, never have a happy moment, never feel joy again, never feel peace or relief again.

I looked around. I wanted to get out of wherever I was. I wanted desperately to wake up from whatever nightmare I was in. How can I still think this is a dream? Would not the pain awaken me? Would not my screams cause someone to come and stir me? If this is not a dream, then it is real. I don't want this to be real. Who would?

I could feel the gradual release of moisture run slowly down the side of my nose and I used the back of my hand to wipe away the tears my eyes managed to squeeze from them. There were remnants of blood now mixed with a putrid liquid.

Putting distance between myself and that madman, I slowly half dragged myself farther down the spiral descent. The thick air made it hard to breathe as the climate continued to climb in temperature and denseness. How could I be lumped together with that man? Bad things don't happen to good people. If that were true, then why in Hell was I there? I'm so lost! "I don't want to be alone!" I whispered. I wanted the pain to end. My suffering was greater than what I would even deem for my enemy.

# 32

## Crazy?

"Let me die!" I screamed once I saw the blinding fluorescents again.

If I died here, then I could just go to Heaven and be done with this whole crazy mess. I ached all over, much like I had felt in the past when I had influenza. All I had to do was let go, surrender my life to death. I was weak enough and tired enough that it would be easy to slip away.

I could move again. No one stood over me. The doctor and my husband were gone. I was almost glad that they were not there. I didn't like the way they felt it necessary to whisper around me. I wish I had heard them plainly so that I did not have to keep guessing.

I looked in the direction of the other patient and saw the same old woman sitting on her bed still rocking. She stopped as if she knew I was looking at her. She turned and looked at me. Her hair was white and to her shoulders; it was as disheveled as anyone's hair is in a hospital. She wore a robe over her hospital gown. Softly, she rose from her bed and stepped closer and closer to me. I could hear the scraping of her slippers against the linoleum floor. When she reached my bed side, she looked into my eyes. "You're not crazy," she whispered.

"What's that supposed to mean?" I asked.

What was that supposed to mean? 'I'm not crazy.' If I'm not crazy, then she definitely is. I thought about it a while longer, processing it over and over what this old woman had said to me. Why would she even say that to me? Was I talking in my sleep? Did she know that I had contemplated my sanity and whether I was still retaining it or not?

Is this a dream? Am I still in the cave dreaming of this place? God, what are the answers?

I looked at her more clearly, or tried to look at her more clearly. It took effort to focus on her at all. My mind kept racing back and forth from everything that I had experienced. I must focus. I must know what she meant. There had to be more to what she wanted to say. Her eyes felt deceptively soft and almost caring, yet I knew better. She did not care, no one did. Not even here, but I was okay with that here. I just wanted the suffering to end.

She leaned in closer and answered, "If the truth is that you're not crazy, then the truth must be that . . ."

# 33

## Dead?

Her voice faded in the distance. "What's the truth? If I'm not crazy, then where am I?"

A cavern at the next turn revealed a group of young women vomiting. Their skin was the only thing covering their bones, and yet, there they were forcing whatever was left in them out. The only things left in them were organs, blood vessels, muscles, tissue, etc. This is what decorated the floor. It made me want to vomit, but I fought it back.

They were surrounded by four large mirrors and they paused after each stomach hurl to look in a mirror. Their reflections were distorted, and I could see what they saw. They were huge, by far the largest people I had ever seen! Each woman would scream and cry in frustration. Each in their turn would step back to the group, joining them in throwing up all over the cavern floor.

Turning away, I walked on.

What had that woman said? That I'm 'not crazy.' What is this if it is not crazy? She had begun to tell me. Why had I transported at that time back here? Why could I not stay in a place long enough to get the answer that I asked for?

I do not want to know the truth. The truth will be too much for me. This might be so, but I think I still want to know the truth regardless. Don't I?

I wondered how I was able to move with the amount of pain in my leg that I felt with each step. Crushed bone was held together by torn tissue and separated muscle, and yet, I pursued the idea that there was an end to this, a way out. I drove myself mad with the idea that there had to be a way out. I limped along with no support, nothing to hold on to except the walls that I would not touch, as I did previously and had suffered for it.

I wanted to quit. I wanted to give up and die. Something would not let me. The pain was so much. My leg had swollen to twice its normal size. I knew the blood flow had stopped soon after the incident. I knew the nerves had been severed in several places. But it didn't matter. I could still feel the pain, and it only got worse.

Undistinguished yelling emitted further down. I was going to have to face someone or something else. I didn't want to continue. I did not want to see anyone else. If I had to remain alone, I wanted to be alone. Everyone I came in contact with took me that much deeper into despair. How could I feel more despair than I am already feeling? Somehow it is possible.

I avoided a mound of skeleton pieces, possibly making up five whole persons, which were piled at the base of the tunnel wall. The pile of bones emitted a sorrowful moan. Is that what will become of me?

As I slowly rounded down closer to whoever was shouting louder than the moans from the skeletons, I could hear a woman ranting.

"I have money! Lots of money! I'll pay you to show me or even tell me the way out of here. You'll be a billionaire. I'll give you everything I own, just show me the way out. Let me out of here! How dare you keep me here! I'm worth billions! Why won't you do the smart thing and take my money and get me out?"

I could hear her crying. She wailed like everyone else here. With all her money, she was still trapped here like everyone else. When I finally could see her, her back was to me. From behind I could see she was dressed in expensive clothes. She looked young. She turned around when she heard me. It is difficult to be quiet with one leg being dragged along.

"I'll pay you anything," she pleaded and ran up to me. My condition must have been unseen in her eyes. She continued to beg. "Show me the way out!" She grabbed my shoulders, and her hands felt like needles against my skin.

I shook myself free. I had not responded. I tried to continue. I don't know why I insist to try to push past these people. They always stop me.

"How dare you keep me here!" she shouted. "I should be kept in a nice hotel. I can afford it. I could get you a room, too. Just let me out of here!"

I turned toward her. She was young. Her expensive clothes were torn and dirty. She had a chain attached to her ankle, and though the chain was painted to appear gold, the chain was indeed iron. This time it was I who lashed out physically. I grabbed her and tossed her quite easily against the wall.

"If I knew the way out, do you honestly believe that I would still be here?"

She looked frighten and tears poured down her cheeks. I

didn't care. Suddenly her facial expression completely transformed, and a look of sheer terror and pain etched itself into every muscle of her young face. Her body jerked as if she was trying to dislodge herself from the wall. I then watched as she slowly dissolved, melting into the wall. I had caused that. I had caused her to touch the one thing I wouldn't touch. In my heart, my knowledge, I knew that would happen, and I caused it to someone else. The worst part is I didn't care. It bothered me that I didn't care. I hated myself for doing it, but given the opportunity, I would have done it all over again. I had to silence her.

Limping down a few steps, I could hear a familiar voice crying out from behind me, begging to be taken to the exit. She offered a treasure for her release. It was the very same woman I had just watched melt away. She was trapped in a vicious cycle.

We were all trapped in the cycle. There was no way to stop the cycle. We could plead, grovel, gamble, bribe, and still we remain here. Not one of us wants to be here. Who would? We would all like to fade away, but we cannot. I don't know why we cannot, that is just the way it is.

I don't know how your mind is processing every word, every detail of my existence here. Are you even able to comprehend what I have been telling you? Do you really understand? Can you understand? For your sake, I hope so. Then again, who are you?

I can only imagine that your mind is spinning a fraction of what my thoughts are constantly doing. My brain is on a roller-coaster, while my fears are the driving force. Fear does not end, so the ride does not end. The track—well it's worse than any ride you will ever go on. The clamps for the cars do not work and occasionally you fly off the tracks, slamming into the ground below only for your broken and shattered body to be scraped up and placed back on the track to do it all over again. Sometimes my mind spins so fast, I feel as though I am in orbit. Other times, my emotions are tied to the track while the cars shred them to tatters, driving over them again and again.

I continue. You already know that is all I can do, all I have been doing – continuing. I'm not living, just continuing.

The shadows creep up, at times growing larger until I move a fraction faster. I must stay ahead of them. They must not catch me. I've seen what they can do. You know what they are capable of, too. I know that they will catch up with me. Sooner or later, they will have me in their clutches and tear me apart like they did the others. They will devour me and somehow, by some black magic, I will come together again just so that they can do it all over again. Why am I here?

Each cavern I passed a force prevented me from entering, as though the cavern was not meant for me. Only those belonging to a particular cavern were allowed to enter. I turned a bend in the tunnel and came upon yet another one of these caverns, one that I could only stand on the outside looking in. Men and women were walking around saying things like: 'don't step on the cracks,' 'knock on wood,' 'thirteen is an unlucky number.' Superstition had invaded their thoughts and hearts and they had given more authority to a block of wood that God had made than to the creator Himself. By 'knocking on wood' they told God that He was not big enough to handle the situation.

Some of them would say a prayer and I could tell from their words that they were Christian and then out of the same mouth they would spew a superstition. This surprised me. If they were Christian, why were they here?

Why am I here?

They didn't believe the truth that God is stronger, higher, victor, conqueror. Instead, they believed that God did some nice thing a long time ago and now … what? … He can no longer do the miracles He once did, or save His people. We must now read the stars and see what our horoscope says and what our lucky numbers for the day are. We trust that a block of wood can take away the words we have just said or that we must avoid walking where a black cat has walked or something terrible will happen. Fools!

I believe in God. I did believe. So, why am I here?

A building frustration rose within me. Everyone here got on my nerves. There was not one person here along this tunnel that did not grate every cell of my being. The ones that I hated the most were the Christians that had ended up here because of their disbelief, willful disobedience, and unforgiveness.

"You fools!" I yelled, annoyed to the point of rage at them and their complete stupidity. "What can a crack do to you?" I asked. "A block of wood has no more power than the tree the wood came from. How can wood protect you? It burns when lit; it rots when wet! Don't you get it? Fools! The absurdity!"

My words again fell on deaf ears. Not one of them looked at me. Had they placed their trust in the God who created the wood, then they wouldn't have been here. I stomped away furious. I was angry more at myself, though I was rather annoyed at them, too. I remembered while alive how I, too, had my own superstitions. Every time I gave into the 'good-luck' of a special item, I was telling God that I didn't trust Him to take care of the matter. How stupid I was!

Deaf ears! My words of wisdom not once penetrated the ears of those down here. My words fell by the wayside, not heard by anyone other than me, and I did not need to hear the truth of which I already knew. What good did it do to tell them truth now? What good did it do me to try to tell them? It was clearly too late for any of them. How many of them told me a bit of truth and it not reach my ears? The words could not reach my heart, I did not have one. I had one once, but not anymore.

# Dead?

"Why am I here? Will someone not tell me? I was a good person. So I slipped up from time to time, everyone does. I asked for forgiveness. God forgives. I did much more good than bad. I went to church. I paid my tithes. Why am I here? God, will You not tell me why I am here? Why am I …" I stopped myself before I said the word 'dead.'

I cannot be dead. Though I am clearly walking through death, and this is—well, I won't go there either, I should not be here. I am young, and though the young do die, God protects His children. I had always been called God's child. I know my body is rotten and decaying, but I cannot be dead. This is all a mistake.

A hunger came over me. I had been hungry the entire time, but suddenly a violent hunger possessed my senses. I had to eat. There was nothing to eat. I looked down and saw grubs, billions of grubs. In some cultures grubs are considered food. They looked juicy and fat. Perhaps I could also quench my thirst. Hesitantly, I bent forward and scooped up a handful of grubs. For the first time, the insects did not dissolve my hand, though my hand was pretty much already bone with a few pieces of flesh attached.

I put the grubs hungrily into my mouth and chewed. I wanted to spit them out, but my lips had been sealed the moment I put the insects into my mouth. I cried bitterly as I could feel the acid dissolve my teeth, trickle down my throat, and eat away at my esophagus and then my intestines. The grubs were eating me from the inside out and I had helped them to the feast.

I swayed under the pain. I almost collapsed under the torment. I now knew how the woman felt when she melted into the wall. I felt as though I was melting from the inside. I could not stop it. The pain. God, what did I do to You?

I should stop talking to Him. He doesn't answer. He doesn't care.

Make the pain stop!

I glanced behind me and saw the shadows coming from behind the bend. Instantly, I moved along. If the insects didn't end me those monsters would. Would that be so bad – coming to an end? If I actually came to an end, but I have seen no evidence that it would happen.

I need you to remember the worst pain you have ever felt. Hold on to that pain. Magnify that pain by a hundred, a thousand and you still won't experience a fraction of the intensity of pain I feel here. You cannot fathom it, it is immeasurable, and it is constant. The only way to understand is to join me here. You must also remember that if you join me, it is permanent.

The path had been alive before that moment, moving and changing shape when it needed to. Now, as I stumbled along, I could see that the path was narrowing and the movement had ceased. I could see there were still insects, but they did not move. They were lying in wait for an attack. They were lying in wait for me.

I pressed on … no, pressing on requires willpower. I had no willpower. I had fear, the fear of those insects that wanted me, wanted to devour the rest of me. The ones inside had not completed the task, but the ones here on the ground … on the ground this moment… these could finish the job. That fear danced in my head like ants on a sandwich. My skin crawled without the aid of thousands of bugs. I could not stop the fear. I could burn a hole in my head. All I had to do was place my head against the wall or floor and I could empty my mind of all this pain. Or would I really? From what I had seen, will see, there is no way to end this suffering, no way to forget or burn away the memories.

Is it necessary that I walk through this pain? Is it necessary that I walk through this suffering? Someone once told me that sometimes God makes us walk through pain so that we can learn. Am I being taught something? Tell me the rule or lesson plainly so that I can walk away from this! I desperately need to walk away from this. I cannot live like this.

The path narrows more and more, and I continue. Why can I not stop? I wanted to take my mind out of there, like I had before. Every time it had backfired, but maybe I could get it right this time. I focused on Heaven. Everything I had been taught Heaven was like, I narrowed my thoughts to those descriptions.

# 34

## Heaven?

Suddenly, I was back in the hospital, laying down on a bed. I sat up. "Why am I here? This isn't Heaven!" I pointed out. The beach would have been a closer representation of Heaven than the hospital. I slid my feet from beneath the sheets and allowed my body to slip out of the bed. In my hospital gown, I exited the room and walked down the hall. There was no one else there. Why is this hospital always void of people? I did not consider the doctor, my husband, or even the old woman people. They were empty. Even now, as I think back on the kindness of the old woman, I sensed a second agenda. She had been empty, too, only telling me those things to frighten me and make me second guess my situation. I hated her. I hated them all.

Wandering the halls only proved how alone I was there, too. I just wanted to go to Heaven. I was tired of being alone. The pain was horrible, maddening, but the aloneness, it was by far worse. I want Heaven.

Down the last hallway, I saw a bright light. The light grew larger until it consumed the entire corridor. I started toward the brightest spot, but two hideous beasts, monsters with sharp teeth and a combination scale and fur coat, and three sharp horns on their heads, grabbed me with their sharp claws, holding me back. They did not have shadows. I had a shadow, but they did not. Their presence terrified me. Is this how they really look? These creatures belonged to the Hell reality, not this reality. How did they get here? Their shadows exist in one place, torturing and tormenting the people there, and their physical bodies exist here? What is here? They had finally caught me. I had almost escaped them by fully entering the light, but they caught me.

I was more afraid then than any other time since I began on this alternate reality ride. I already had become fear, and now I was even more afraid. I knew that these monsters were going to tear me apart. Their breath on my neck and shoulders was hotter than the heat of the tunnel. I was desperate for them to let me go. Why were they holding on to me? Let me walk into the light. Why were they not tearing me to pieces as I had seen them do in the cave? Why were they not eating my flesh? Perhaps I no longer had flesh. I looked over at my arms and could see that they were intact, though they did not feel intact.

The light was warm, but not like what I had been exposed to already. It was a wonderful warmth, but it was not welcoming, not to me. The beasts held me even tighter. I could not escape one way or the other, neither forward nor backward. It didn't keep me from struggling in their grip. Terror moved me. I needed out, away from the beasts, away from the light.

I never felt so filthy, so undeserving of anything than I did of that light. I could not go into the light even if the beasts released me. The shame I had been experiencing intensified. I wanted to hide from the light. I wanted the light to go away. I could no longer bear to even look at it. I closed my eyes tight. It had to go away. I felt worse than unworthy, I felt completely worthless.

The light was so bright that I could see the light through my eyelids. When I felt that it was dark, I opened my eyes. The light was gone. The monsters were gone, but evidence of the sharpness of their claws was scratched into my arms. I stood alone in the tunnel.

# 35

## Closed

I had wanted Heaven, but Heaven had been closed to me. How could Heaven be closed to me? Why not? Everything else I had thought of had been closed. Perhaps everything I knew about Heaven was false. It could just be that I was unable to call it into existence because I had never been there and did not really know what Heaven is really like. I don't know. I just don't know. It had been closed to me.

I do know! If Heaven is closed to me then that can only mean that I'm not dead. I can only go to Heaven if I am dead. So, I'm not dead. How can I not be dead? And why am I here? Even with this new revelation, I do not find comfort.

But I am dead. I have to be. No one living can survive this. It is impossible. My heart isn't even beating. My lungs stopped filling up with air long ago or was it a few minutes ago I stopped breathing?

Tell me, why am I here? Do you know where here is? Have you figured it out already? I cannot grasp it. The truth fails to imprint itself on me. It fails to make the connection with my brain. I cannot fathom it. The truth is like a complex equation that is unsolvable. As hard as I try, I cannot get an answer, and yet the truth is also as simple as one plus one.

Constant vertigo, heat searing the skin off my tissue and muscle, bone scraping bone and grinding against nerves, razor sharp shards slicing into my feet with every step, insects chewing on the wounds of my feet and the insides of my body, yet I keep going. Please don't make me keep going. I can't keep going. I'm not even going. I stopped at the top of this abyss. Evil moved me. Evil carried me down farther and farther.

"Leave me alone!" I shouted to whatever would hear me, whatever would listen. "Just let me stop! Leave me alone!"

I wiped away the blood stained tears. I was now dotted with more of my own blood. My shirt, my arms, my back, my feet, my face, all had blood smeared on them, mixed with tears, sweat, vomit, and even bile. Dust from the dead and insects were also a mixture of the grime that stained my body. Never in my life had I ever come close to being this vile. I was vile. I was pain. I had become death, not just dead, but death.

I kept going. I even tried locking my legs into place, refusing to take a step. Tapping into a stubbornness I didn't know I could possess, willing to allow … willing for the beasts to come and do their worst and possibly end this. It didn't work. I began to lean forward. The steps tilted forward almost causing me to fall. The steps had tilted just so that I had to continue. I took a step and the stairs straightened out. Not even the ground would give me rest.

# 36

# A Stream

A pungent odor attacked my olfactory sense. It always smells bad, but this was, for the moment, an addition to the already nauseating air.

Have you smelled death – a decaying animal on the side of the road or out in the woods? Because everything here is death, you are surrounded by the smell. Almost immediately your clothes begin to smell like death, your hair begins to smell like death, your skin begins to smell like death, and even your breath begins to smell like death. You cannot get away from it.

Have you seen buzzards or crows or insects eating a dead animal? The buzzards, crows and insects remove the dead animal from the face of the earth, so that you don't have to be bothered by it for long. There are no buzzards or crows here, and the insects become part of you, not really consuming you to nonexistence, but instead while they are eating you they are also piecing you back together just so that they can continue eating you for eternity.

The brew of rotting flesh, sulfur, methane, and burnt skin and hair encompassed the air. As I wound down, I could see that the walls and floor were wet ahead. The smell had been coming from that liquid. By now, it was bright enough for me to see that it was a stream of blood. The stream ran down one wall, across the floor and up the other. The ceiling seemed to be the only thing untouched by the blood.

Do you remember the moaning bones? This stream was not silent either. It sounded like the wailing of billions of infants. It was the echo of the voices of murdered babies and children. Those who did not have a voice to cry out while alive, begging for a chance to live, now had a voice, a voice that torments all those who stole their lives, all those who hear. We all hear.

Guilt fell over me for every one of those babies. I had never even raised a hand to a child, and yet I felt as though I had been the one that had killed each one. A bitter cry erupted from my heart. Their voices were echoes, shadows of the real thing. The real thing was not here, fortunate for them, but their voices … their voices stung the heart. The guilt paralyzed me. I could not move. I didn't want to move. I needed to move.

Ignoring the pain of guilt the best I could, I brought my attention back to the fact that the stream blocked the tunnel. I had to keep moving. I could not be stopped here.

I did not know how deep the stream of blood was, and I really didn't want to find out. I didn't want to step in it, so I skipped quickly down the steps heading up to it and on the last dry step I leapt, pushing hard off the step, and dreading what would happen if I hadn't pushed hard enough. I landed hard on my broken leg. I hadn't pushed hard enough. My broken leg had not made it all away across the blood spring, landing feet away from dry ground.

I slipped, my legs sliding out from beneath me. Covered in blood and crashing down the stairs, I slammed into the walls. With each touch to the volcanic heated walls, my own flesh melted away, burning off. My clothes were burned and torn, and now clung to my beaten, battered body.

I eventually stopped falling and landed in the middle of the tunnel. Lying there, with broken bones sticking out from various parts of my body—I could even see a rib sticking out of my side—and looking up, I could see that there was an open cavern above me. In the cavern, I saw five bodies hanging from nooses. Each person still kicked about, gasping for air, though this air would not bring much relief. Even though they were two hundred feet above me and the lighting was dull at best, I could see their eyes. Each of them were looking down at me, begging me to rescue them from the torture. I could not. I did not want to. I did not need to.

I rolled over on my stomach, and with my hands I pushed myself to a semi-standing position. I rocked back and forth on my legs just to remain balanced. If I paused for more than a couple of seconds, I, myself, would begin to lean, not the steps this time, and I would topple over.

Broken was too light a word to describe me, let alone my position. I felt I had been put through a wood chipper and then glued back together, though not with ordinary glue, ... no ... no, ordinary glue would not work, ... it had to be blood, the blood of many others. I lifted my shirt and could see my lung right through my cracked ribs. The skin and tissue had been seared away. I don't think there was one bone in my body that was not cracked, broken or crushed. I was a broken vessel, beyond repair.

How could I be alive? People don't go through this and live, let alone remain conscious. I was conscious. I was aware of everything around me. I didn't understand, nor wanted to understand what was going on. They say 'the truth shall set you free,' but here, that is an impossibility. Here, the truth makes you that much more a prisoner, and yet, settling on lies will not free you either. You can never be free here. This is the ultimate prison.

'Why is there so much death? Anyone care to speculate?' I don't want to guess. I don't want to be right and I don't want to be wrong. And yet, does it really matter? I am here.

I had to be crazy. No one sane would create these visions before me. No one sane would be in this mess. A sane person could get out of it. Couldn't they? I had to get out of it. Why was I there?

A boy emerged from a wall and proceeded to run across the path. He stopped in the middle of the stairs, looked at me, screamed, "You're hideous!" and continued running. I knew he was right. My hair was falling out. The flesh from my feet and hands were eaten away. My shoes had completely melted away. My clothes were torn, pieces ripped off. My shoulder blade had a bone jabbed in it. My side had a rib poking out. Blood stained my clothes and my leg swelled to twice its normal size. The same boy came back through the wall and turned to me again. "Follow me, I'll show you the way out!"

A way out! Could it be possible? I wanted to believe him. I needed to believe him. I had to believe him. I believed him. I needed to believe him, but most importantly, he needed to be telling me the truth. He ran ahead down the spiral steps. I hobbled fast enough for a slow jog. With each step, the intense pain had every opportunity to force me into a dead faint.

Instead, it kept me conscious, torturing me with the slightest motions.

At first, I could see the boy just one step before the turn would hide him from me. With his agility and my infirmity, I lost sight of him.

"Slow down! I can't keep up," my voice gurgled, blood and other liquid or bone in my lungs preventing me from speaking clearly. I limped on. "Please wait!"

He was gone. I had to rest. The pain I had to bear, could not share it, no one willing to take it from me or end me, broke me to a mass of self-loathing and despising my very existence. I had stopped in front of a cavern and had to lean on the wall for support. I wanted my body to melt into the wall, but I didn't. Instead, I had rested the bone sticking out from the shoulder blade on the wall. It heated, and then sent a surge of heat throughout my body, cooking me from the inside. I hurt to move and not to move. So for the moment, I chose not to move.

Inside this cavern, plastered on every wall, were pictures. I decided to see what they were of, so for the first time, I ventured into one of the side caves. I had been able to step into this cave. Revolted, my eyes appallingly glanced from one picture to another. It was child pornography. Why would anyone allow for someone to put up these pictures? Anyone who would have these up should be in jail. Am I in a prison?

A giggle behind me forced me to turn around. The boy was holding hands with some man. The man's features were skewed uglier than any of the once human beings I had crossed so far. Blood drained from his eyes, mouth and nose. The boy smiled as they turned and headed through the wall.

"Wait! Don't go with him! He's a bad man!" They didn't listen. They walked through the wall. I didn't bother to try and follow. I didn't care. The boy had lied to me, deceived me about a way out. I tried to warn him, but he chose not to listen. I left the cavern . . .

# 37

## Surgery

. . . and entered the hospital. Why couldn't I stay in one place?

I was standing. I was in an operating room. Doctors and nurses were standing around a person in the middle of surgery. No one noticed that I was there. I looked at the person they were cutting open. I looked at myself. Turning away . . .

# 38

## Confusion

I took each step slowly. This was all a dream. I must have been climbing with my husband. I wondered into a cave, got hurt. I was taken to the hospital, and I'm stuck in this dream while they try and fix me. My fear of closed in places has concocted this horrible, but elaborate nightmare, to force me to make the decision as to whether I get better or not. All these creatures must be distractions, barriers to keep me from getting to the bottom of this cave. When I get to the bottom, I'll get better. Now, this is plausible. It has to be. I can't live like this the rest of my life.

Am I alive?

# 39

## What Now?

I stood in the hall of the hospital again. Still alone. No one to be seen or heard. I reached for a room door, but it was locked. I peeped through a small window in the door and saw the old woman sitting on a bed closest to the outer wall. She was looking away from me. I glanced back at the end of the hall. There was nothing but more rooms, more doors. The end of the hallway ended with a set of double doors.

I glanced back up at the window to the door I had tried to open. To my horror the woman's face was now smashed against the pane and her eyes stayed on me.

"You're not crazy!" she taunted. "This isn't a dream!"

I stumbled while backing away from the door. She was too scary to believe. She looked crazy herself. I wanted out of all of it. I needed to get out of there. My gaze rested at the end of the hall on the set of double doors.

The lights flickered as if the power were failing. One particular light, which flickered the most, hung over the double doors at the end of the hall. This turned all my attention to the red letters that lit up the Emergency sign. That one word in this instance seemed to warn me of a coming danger, that is, if I wasn't already in danger. How would I know? I had to see for myself.

Once again, I took a step toward the Emergency Room. A curiosity came over me that I couldn't fight off. I wanted to see what was behind the door. Would I see myself again or would I see the invisible beast that had chased me earlier? Maybe, just maybe, what was behind the door could help me, would help me, instead of causing me harm and more pain.

Why did I have to be wrong? So completely wrong! When I was halfway down the hall, a creature burst from the Emergency Room. It had a strong, flexible body and limbs; its mouth revealed thorn-like teeth; its tail was decorated with sharp spikes ready to pierce my body. I froze. I stared at it. I could see that it wanted me to run. It was a predator and I was its prey. It took a step toward me. It growled, flashing its teeth. I didn't wait. I could see that whether I ran or not, it was going to attack me. I turned and ran with the adrenaline that is released in the chased. It thundered a roar that vibrated even the floor and then bounded after me.

This was the second time I wanted the hospital reality or nightmare or whatever to end. For the first time, I wanted to be back in the cave and to remain there. Which was worse: a couple of shadow monsters that would tear me apart, yet I wouldn't die, or a carnivorous beast chasing me down to devour me and chances are I won't make it? This could be my chance to end this. But the fear of death and the afterlife which awaits caused my legs to run away and I could not will them to stop.

Why was this beast in the hospital? I had never before in my life seen anything which remotely resembled it.

I ran around the first corner and down another long hallway. The bounding of the beast shook the floor; this made me disoriented, but I still ran on. Adrenaline surged through my body, offering me a chance to outrun the predator. Upon the next corridor, I opened the door to the stairwell and spiraled down the steps. To my disappointment and fear, the beast followed me, easily catching up to me. It took a swing at me with its paw. The claws ripped my shirt and tore through my arm. Again, it swung and caught me in the head, tearing out my hair and leaving me with part of my face dangling at my neck.

"I want to go back to the cave!" I screamed, falling forward, since I could no longer see with the blood pooling in my eyes, blinding me. I rolled down the stairs; the beast pursued. Bones cracked and ligaments, tissue, and muscles tore on the impact of my body with stair, railing, wall, and occasionally claw.

I landed with my face smashed against the corner of a step. Hoisting myself up from the rocky path, I could have kissed the ground, but knew my lips would disintegrate. Then it hit me. No matter which reality I became a part of, I was trapped in misery and suffering. Hate, anger, and anguish would remain with me. The horror of the elements and any creatures I stumbled upon would only haunt me and cause me more suffering. And worse, I could not die! I could not end the suffering. I was stuck in an evil, eternal cycle.

# 40

# The Tunnel

Despair dragged me down farther and farther into the nothingness that laid in wait for me. I couldn't believe that life or death could get any worse. A warm breath sent a tingling sensation to the back of my neck. Had I failed to discern another being slither up behind me? I didn't want to move. I didn't want to face it. Stopping dead in my track, I slowly turned around, looking at the ground all the while. Lifting my head, my eyes widened once I gazed upon the ghastly sight. This creature looked like death itself, that is, if death had a look. The woman floating within inches of me appeared to be covered in a black mass of hair-like quality. The wild, sunken eyes staring back at me unnerved my very soul. She was wild, unstable, and angry. The same could be said of me at that moment.

Neither of us moved, me from fright, and her ... well ... I don't know what her reason was. To frighten me I suppose. It worked. In a slow steady voice the woman in black said, "You know where you are, but you choose not to accept it," as if reading my thoughts. "I, too, do not accept it. This is a trick; it's not real. Nothing here is real. This place does not exist." She repeated to me the very words I had been saying all along.

I was right. It was all a delusion. But how could I get out of it? What did this woman represent in my delusion? Or maybe I'm apart of someone else's delusion. No! Who am I kidding? I'm trying to make sense of something that—well I'm trying to take a truth that I believed to be a lie and make it into something that makes sense. But, the only thing that makes sense is the truth. I can't face the truth. I can't face the reality. But this woman, I could tell that she was going to tell me what I didn't want to hear.

Her eyes scanned my face, or what I presumed must have been left of my face, for I knew that my face had to begin to look like the rest of me. Was she reading my thoughts and fears? She must have, for she said, "There are those here that say this place is Hell, but if it were Hell then there would be a Heaven, and I don't believe in Heaven, or God, or Satan, so this place is simply a nightmare that I am forced to never wake from."

"No! This can't be Hell. Hell doesn't exist! Or if it does, it's for people who are bad. Not for good people. I've been good!" I looked at the ground, though I suppose I should have looked up. "Dear God, help me." I whispered. A nightmare never to wake from? What does that mean? Am I, too, stuck in this nightmare? No, this is a trick. She's tricking me. She's just repeating all those things that I've been playing over and over in my own mind. I wanted to scream and found that I couldn't. A reality was trying to settle itself in me. I didn't believe in that reality. There is no way that I was really there. I couldn't accept that. I wouldn't accept that. But, the reality was I could feel the flames even though I couldn't see them. Insects covered my hands and feet. Burns covered me in rash-like patches. Somehow, I stood as stationary as the ghost woman in front of me.

The woman looked at me, stared blankly into my eyes. "The truth is this place cannot exist, because God does not exist. Has he answered your cries? No! He never has and he never will."

I found my voice. "You're as crazy as the rest of them here," I cried. But she had been right. God did not answer my callings, my cries, my pleas, my prayers.

All the woman had to say in reply was, "Crazy is the only thing that makes sense."

I've said that, too. Moving even closer to me, the woman floated right through me like the little girl had. The sensation was just like before. I felt as though she was tearing me apart, and for what, just to get past me. She could have just walked around me, but no—I knew what she was thinking as she walked through me. If she had chosen to walk around me, then she would be accepting that this place is real. Fool! "This place is real!" I cried. This pain could not be made up. This fear could not be a mere thought. I am not crazy.

There I was back to crazy. I had to be crazy. Crazy was better than reality, at least this one. But why was I there? Why could I feel pain? Why couldn't it just all end? But, there is no end to eternity.

"God, if You do exist, why am I trapped in this asylum? How could You let me, a good person, fall into such a dismal place? I've never done anything to warrant this. Why am I crazy? God, are You listening?!" I pleaded to the air.

He continued to remain silent. People in the Bible heard His voice. People at church had heard His voice. There were even times when I believed that I, too, had heard His voice, leading me, guiding me, directing my decisions. Here, I heard nothing. He kept His voice closed to me. I don't know why He would choose now to be silent, now that I was willing to hear, willing to listen.

So alone. So empty. I felt so alone.

I want you to imagine your greatest fear, the most frightening thing you can picture. If you're a phobic, this should be easy for you. Now, I want you to magnify that feeling by double, triple. Even if you could guess what it would feel like intensified by a hundred percent, you could not come close to the terror I've experienced in one second down here. I know all the answers now. I know why people don't want to believe this place exists. I know why people want to believe that good works will keep you out of here. I also now know that most people believe in lies. Being good won't cut it. Doing good things and hoping that your good will outweigh your bad will not keep you from spending eternity here. Believing that this place doesn't exist will not make this place disappear. In fact, it only makes this place all that more horrifying when you do end up here. If you denied the truth while alive, you walk in that very denial here unable to accept what you see and hear and feel, and yet you know that you are facing truth and judgement.

I'm here, trapped with iniquity itself. I'm not supposed to be here. I should be in Heaven. Why am I not in Heaven? I know that this is a test. I know that at any moment I will be alive and given a second chance. God made a mistake. I should not be here. How did I get here?

# 41

## Am I Dead?

I suddenly felt overwhelmingly cold and looked down at my body to see what was happening. I was naked. I wasn't standing which startled me into action, as I threw out my arms to brace myself. My arms did not have far to move, banging them almost instantly into the metallic cold walls which now surrounded me. I was flat on my back and when I repositioned my head to look forward, and in this case up, I could see the ceiling inches from my nose. It, too, was metallic. The container I was in felt like a fridge, cold air poured into the space from a small vent behind my head. The only light seeped in from a crack at my feet. I inched my way down swaying side to side and scooting with every joint that proved useful. Once I was close enough, I kicked hard and the end of the freezing cage opened. Continuing to scoot out, I finally found myself standing in a morgue.

"Are you crazy?!" I screamed, realizing what had happened. "I am still alive!"

No one answered.

I stood there with my mind spinning. It dawned on me what I had just said: I am still alive. Have I been given the second chance I expected?

A second before, I had accepted that I was dead, or had I? If I was, then why did I keep coming back here? The last time I was here, I was attacked by a beast which tore me to pieces. That should have killed me if I had been alive. I felt the pain, so I must have been alive. Right? Dead people don't feel pain. That is what I have been told my whole life.

I looked down at my naked body and could not find any evidence that I had been attacked by a beast. I was, however, startled to see the Y-incision sloppily stitched up on my torso. If I am dead, why am I here? What am I supposed to get out of seeing all of this? Am I supposed to come to terms and accept that I am dead and stuck in Hell? Who would accept that?

If I am dead, then why am I here?

Here is better than Hell. Or is this, too, Hell? The questions, they don't stop, and there are no answers, no acceptable ones.

I walked forward, toward a set of doors. I hesitated to open them, the memory of my previous attempts at double doors fresh in my thoughts, taunting me to open the doors at my own risk, and risk I will face.

However, I did open them, and even more, I stepped through them, not concerned who might see me completely exposed. I didn't know what to expect when I opened the door. I did expect that anything could and might happen. I even expected that I might transport myself back to the hell-hold of the tunnel. I'm not sure if I had been prepared for what did happen.

172

I stepped into a mist of web. The sensation of the web on my body sent shivers down my spine and I immediately tried to wipe off the web. However, the further I stepped into wherever, for I could not see further than a foot in front of me, the thicker the web mist was. All around me was white, a thick cloud of silk threads surrounded me. I could no longer see the doors I had stepped through. The webs clung to me, at first, merely lacing me in the silk threads, and soon clothed me completely in the sticky, spidery substance. The web around me began to wrap me like a mummy. The idea of the spider or the amount of spiders to create this web distressed me beyond what my nerves could handle. The web surrounded my head and was closing off my facial features: my eyes, my mouth, my ears, my nose. I could not breathe.

I tried to shake myself loose from the web, but it only seemed to cause the web to grow thicker around me. I began this delusion incased in a morgue freezer and was now shrouded in the worst mummification process ever conceived. I honestly wanted to be back in the freezer. Death is hell after hell after hell!

Suddenly, even though my ears were thickly covered, I could once again hear the words: "Guilty. You have been found guilty!" I felt the torment of the shame which encompassed me. The web was shame; it shrouded me in its anguish. "You chose your own path, your own understanding. You did not trust the Lord of Hosts. Your heart is cold and death is your judgement."

I wanted to scream out 'how' and 'why' but found that I could not. The voices faded, yet I remained trapped in the web —the web of my shame, the web of my own deceit, the web of my own creation.

For a second, between heartbeats, I swore I could hear something, as though I was not alone. I tried to yell again, but only managed a muffled moan. Then I could distinctly feel eight parts of my body being pressed. My imagination drew out in my mind the size of the spider that had me in its possession. My body tensed up at first and then began to spasm uncontrollably. Then a pain like no other shot through my stomach. I had been impaled. The object that had been stuck in me felt smooth and hot and smaller than I had envisioned; it also felt familiar. I could soon feel a burning sensation serge through my body, and I imagined the poison that must be pumping through my blood stream, attacking my nervous system.

Initially I felt drunk, then all my joints locked up and my muscles tightened. My muscles grew tighter and tighter and I knew they were going to snap off my bones. My head pounded and my heart raced and then began to slow.

I could feel warmth all over me and I could feel the web melting off of me. Someone was melting the web off of me. 'Wait! Go slower! I'm still alive,' I thought but could not say. The heat required to melt the web could be felt to my bones. With the last strain of web melted off, I was again in the tunnel.

"I'm not alive. I am dead." I voiced. "I wish I can die in death. Perhaps, I would not be here. I don't mind not being," I cried. Still no comfort; no peace.

# 42

## I Am Dead

This time as I followed the abyss, it was with some accepted revelation, at least in regard to where I was. I still could not accept that I was here on purpose. It had to all be a mistake. I, of all people, should not be here. I had heard testimonies of people who had been sent here by God in dreams or in near death experiences, only to be brought back to their homes or hospital beds. I knew, or wanted to believe that at any moment, I would be whisked away from here. That I would open my eyes and all of this would have been a warning. Though for the life of me ... what a joke ... life ... I tormented myself ... for all of existence, I could not fathom what I was being warned against. That this place exists? Did I not already know that? I guess in the back of my mind I figured that since Heaven existed then this place must exist, too. I was a good person; I did good things, more good than bad. I had not earned this.

"So this place exists. I know this now." I waited. "God, You can take me away from here." I waited longer. What was He proving? What did He want me to know?

I wanted to hope, but I could not remember how to hope. This place strips you of hope. I wanted to physically cling to a hope that I would get out of here somehow. This all had to be a mistake. Does God make mistakes? I never thought so until now. I should not be here.

"What are You teaching me, God?"

I realized that I was talking to Him again. God has not answered me; He is not going to answer me. Why do I keep talking to Him? He doesn't even hear me! He hates me! For some reason, He hates me and has put me here. Why? O, Lord, what did I ever do to deserve this?

The floor no longer had to encourage me to continue. Some unseen force dragged me deeper, pulling me by every hair, nerve, and loose flesh. If I stopped, the pain would intensify, though I think it was all in my head. When I stopped, I focused more on the pain than when I walked.

Yet, you must know the pain is always present and hurts more and more every moment. You must understand that this doesn't end. It goes on for eternity. You understand time, but time does not exist, not here. Forever means forever, no limit, no boundary, no point A to point B. You cannot escape. There is no way out. You search and search, but all you find is agony, evil, and disgust. You loathe your existence as much as you loathe everyone else. You cannot escape your emotions; they drag on with you, intensifying at every turn. Your emotions deceive you, and bring you physical pain. Your body rots, burns, breaks, tears, is eaten, yet you continue to be, not living. As I have said before, you are not alive, you just are, you continue. There is no death after death, no end. You can scream as loud as you want, as long as you want, but it will do no good. Yet, you cannot help but scream. The pain is too intense to hold back the wailing, the tears, the moaning, the screams, but no one will listen, and those who do hear you do not care. I don't care. If you are so foolish to follow me, or to even think that by your own good deeds you will somehow escape this, you are a bigger fool than I am.

I have family here. They cannot comfort me. We are forever separated, knowing that we are here, here in this same place of torment and torture, yet we cannot ever see each other. You have family and friends here, if you are foolish enough to join them, you, too, will never see them. Your misery will never have company. You will never be comforted.

# 43

## Demons of Darkness

I paused but could not stand still. I had to keep moving. Will I be walking on like this forever? Ever moving, never allowed to rest, always in pain? I knew I would. I could not accept it; my mind would not allow the truth to settle in. There had to be an end.

The atmosphere shifted. There was a presence ahead of me, though I could not discern what kind of presence. Whatever it was thickened the air until it was tangible. You could touch it, hold it, breathe it. It frightened me. I wanted to go back, back to the crazy woman, back to the boy, back to the vomiting women, back to the little girl, back to the witch doctor, back to the entrance. I would gladly remain at the entrance, back into the complete darkness. Did I not tell you that had I only known then what I know now that I would have preferred to remain in the dark? Now you see why.

Suddenly, a wave of flying, transparent beings rushed upon me from every direction. Like a twister, they circled me, pulling me along the cave path. They screeched in my ears and pulled at my tattered clothing. A pants leg fell to the floor, and they persisted to rip off half of my shirt. These were creatures like none I had ever witnessed before. They were not human, though some of them had human-like features. One had the body of a man but the head of a three headed lion. Another had the wings of a falcon but the body of a lizard. Still another had eyes all over its hands, had the feet of a human, and the head and body of a bear. These creatures under different circumstances might have been intriguing, but to me in that moment, they only brought further pain and more fear.

I could feel myself giving in again to the helplessness, agony and complete depression. Over and over I relented to the pain, the emptiness, the fear. All of these emotions and sensations continually increased. There was no peak, no point where I could not feel worse, where I had reached the worst. There was always increase, always more pain. I could not break the cycle. I wanted these spirits, these creatures to leave me alone. I could not fight back. My arms would go right through them, however, they were able to grab me and pull. I was a puppet and they were pulling the strings. These strings, however, were attached permanently and were pieces of my body and clothing. I had no control. No other once-human creature had control over me, not like this, but they—they had control. I relinquished the control to them. I had to. I could not stop them. They took authority over me as though I did not have the right to my own body, my own will. I might have at one point—a point before I ended up here, but now … now it was too late. Now, I was in their territory, their home and I had to abide by their demands.

I began to whisper over and over, "God, just let me die. Please, let me die. I don't wish to go on living. I don't care anymore about life. God, let me die."

As soon as I spoke those words, another creature appeared from around a jetting rock. The ghoul stopped me in my tracks, and the ghosts, or whatever they were, rose to the ceiling and carried on their circular flight above my head. I found no comfort in seeing this thing even if it had been the cause of the demons dispersing from around me. The unnatural features surpassed the other monsters I had seen in visual disgust. Bones and flesh and hair stood in a pile before me as though it had all just come through a meat grinder. The foul odor in the air had increased in potency. The smell was intoxicating, gnawing at my olfactory sense down to the pit of my stomach. It nauseated me to the point of throwing up, and when there was absolutely nothing left to come up, I continued to heave.

Then it spoke. "Are you suffering?" The mouth or lips on this being could not be found among the mass of body parts, yet there was discernable noise rising from it.

Staring blankly, I could hardly believe that anyone could be concerned about me in such a place. I certainly did not care about anyone. I took a moment to compile my emotions, which had grown more than merely oversensitive from the stress caused by this place. "I am suffering most horribly," I finally replied. "I'm afraid. I'm lost, and I'm in so much pain." I confessed. "I don't know why I am here. I don't belong here."

Confession I thought was supposed to make you feel better. I only felt worse. I wouldn't have to wait long to find out why.

"Good!" it shouted in my direction. Utterly alone, I could no longer be shocked by what I saw or heard. How could anyone care, anyone that was here, too? "I draw pleasure from your suffering. You know what they say: Misery loves company? It's not true here. Everyone here hates everyone else. No one loves anyone or anything. Love cannot exist here. This place is what the absence of love really looks like. There is only one love and most people never find it."

Well, I had been right all along. I now had confirmation that we all hated each other. We would gladly leave everyone behind to suffer only to stop suffering ourselves.

The selfishness that built up within me became as cold as my stony heart. I carried bricks inside of me, cold heavy bricks, bricks which represented my cold heart, my selfishness, my lack of caring, my fear, my hopelessness, my pain. I'm probably being redundant here, but I need you to know that I claimed the selfishness, the fear, the hopelessness, the darkness, the evil. I claimed it, and I became it. I had known people who had claimed fears, claimed illnesses, claimed depression, and even claimed death. If you claim it, call it yours, it becomes yours. You've allowed it to attach itself to you. You become it.

You still have the chance to cut those ties. Don't wait until you are here and the ties have you bound for eternity.

The grotesque figure released a heavy sigh, at least all the body parts lifted up and dropped like a sigh; some of the pieces fell off on descent and onto the floor: a finger, tongue, and part of an intestine from what I could make out. The insects immediately attacked the pieces. "I should not be here," it said.

I understood what the blob meant, "I shouldn't be here either," I remarked, repeating what I had already said to it, though I was speaking more to myself, knowing that it was not listening to me.

The mound of human parts ignored my remark again as I had expected. "In the world of the living, I was a minister, a pastor, whatever you care to call it. It doesn't matter now," it sighed again, as if shrugging off a memory that now only brought painful thoughts. "Every Sunday, I stood before my congregation, telling them all about God and how to get to Heaven.

They were all formulas: do this and this and you'll get to heaven. One plus one equals two. Every Sunday, I led them astray, farther and farther from God."

I wanted to interrupt, wanted to get away from all of it, but there was no way past the figure; there was no way out, there never was. Why did I have to listen to all these people? What was the purpose? They didn't tell me anything I couldn't figure out on my own. They didn't teach me anything. All they did was share their misery with me and I just didn't care. I didn't want any part of them. What is the point? I didn't want to hear anymore, but I was forced to wait and listen to all it had to say.

"The formulas were all lies. There was a boy in my church who had a terminal illness. For weeks, I prayed with him and told him he would go to Heaven and be one of God's angels. It was all lies. I don't even know if I believed in the lies or not. He believed. He died and I continued teaching the same formulas and lies. You know what's worse than not believing there is a God?"

The ex-pastor finally drew my attention, "What?" I asked.

"Not knowing that you don't believe."

This sent shivers down my spine, though I wasn't entirely convinced I still had a spine.

"I thought that I believed. There were times that I knew I believed and would one day go to Heaven, but even with all of that, I never received Jesus as my Lord and Savior, never believed that He died on the cross for my sins, never believed that He loved me. I only became a pastor because my father was one and it was expected of me. I knew that I would be respected as a pastor and I did want to do good. The road to hell really is paved with good works and good intentions." He cried.

I watched as the pile of human confetti moistened, becoming gooier than it already had been.

"There is no relief in death, he continued. "Death does not solve problems. It only creates more. The depressed are trapped in a misery that is immensely magnified from what they experienced while alive, and this time, there is no out; they cannot kill themselves in death. The drug abusers cannot be satisfied, because there are no drugs. They shake and stumble, scream and slam their fists into their heads, but they can't overcome the desperate need for a fix. The murderers and rapists are haunted by their deeds, and instead of making amends, they continue to do that which sent them down here to begin with. They can't stop, even though their thirst for lust and blood no longer satisfies them but churns their stomachs. Here, those who were psychopaths, those who had no conscience, now have a conscience and are tormented by it. They cannot escape from what they did, regretting every evil action."

I was standing next to a pastor. A pastor had made it down here. I always had held pastors to a higher standard than everyone else. I expected every pastor to go to Heaven. I was wrong. Pastors are only human, just like the rest of us. This one had been spreading lies, false doctrines. He had believed the false doctrines and not the Bible. It's too late now. But I believed, didn't I? I didn't spend too much time reading the Bible, but I had read it, all the way through at least once. If being good isn't good enough, then how does anyone get to Heaven?

He had not finished and interrupting my thoughts, he continued, "After I died, do you know who was waiting for me at the gates of Hell? It wasn't Satan to congratulate me. It was much worse. It was the little boy whom I had told was going to be an angel of the Lord. The demons had tormented him and had seared the dead wings of a vulture to his back. He had wanted

184

to become an angel so bad that he had obsessed about it. It had consumed him and this was his reward. He blamed me for putting him here. He was right to, but I had not forced him to believe me. I merely made the words too enticing to ignore."

The pastor looked around. It looked scared or how a blob of minced meat might look if it were scared. In a whisper, the pastor continued, "He still haunts me. Everywhere I turn, he pops up. Blaming and blaming. Never giving me rest. Never giving me peace. And it's all my fault."

I had just received an answer to most of my questions, but I could not believe it. This is the residence of the father of lies, the devil, Satan. How could I believe this pastor, this pastor who lived his life in lies? And yet, I knew he told the truth. He is now haunted by the truth, the truth which he ignored.

"Is this a dream?" I didn't really want an answer. I knew the truth, but I didn't want to believe it. I received an answer anyway.

"No." The human meat puzzle scattered right before me. Pieces went in every direction.

The spirits moved back around me, scratching, screeching, pulling me on. I limped down the dark spiral steps that led to God knows where. The rock walls oozed and crawled with life that followed my descent. The stairs went on forever with no promise of leading to a way out or anywhere better than where I had come from. The farther I went, the more painful my body felt. The air ran more toxic. The shrieks of utter misery became more deafening. Besides being drawn onward, my only reason for taking each step farther down was the knowledge that behind me was complete hopelessness.

I tried to look back to see if the shadows were approaching, but the demons would not let me. They directed my every movement.

The spirits scattered after a while, growing tired of taunting me. They would come back. I knew it. These spirits would go throughout Hell tormenting each individual who ended up here. They took turns with the shadow monsters, feeding on our fears and tearing each of us apart. It was their reward for turning away from God long ago. They neither felt gratification nor contentment in their unending role in Hell. They hated God more than anyone else here. They, too, felt pain and could not stop it any better than I could.

My stomach roared with hunger, but there was nothing to eat. My throat, dry, longed for water; there was nothing to drink. I had this unsettling feeling that I would never find nourishment and neither would I die from hunger nor dehydration. I would be left to wander these caves for all eternity. My companions would be hopelessness, fear, and abandonment.

No one can understand what it means to feel this alone, not until they have reached this most undesirable place themselves. The negative emotions overwhelm you, taking over your thoughts, weaving their way into your genetic makeup, making you into a creature of agony, abandonment, hate, fear, and hopelessness.

Panicking, I tried to ignore what the pastor had said. What did he know anyway? I was a good person. God wouldn't send me here. Maybe this was just a test or all a misunderstanding. If I were dead, I should be in Heaven. So, I can't be dead. But, why am I here? A scratching at my leg redirected my thoughts. On my injured leg, insects crawled all over it. They ate away at the flesh revealing muscle and torn tissue. As hard as I could, I swiped at the bugs to get them off. It was a fruitless effort: the insects continued to chew. I released the blood that had fought to flow out of my eyes. Pain, I'm sure, was etched over ever feature of my body. The groaning vibrated off the rocks and I stumbled as another earthquake-like sensation rattled the stairs beneath my feet. I yelled at the forever continuous noise, "Stop groaning! Stop screaming! Can't you stop?" I covered my ears the best I could. It did no good.

The earthquake strengthened, bouncing me down the stairs at a much faster pace than I cared to go. Ahead the light grew brighter, and I hoped for a moment that I had finally found a way out of this hellish nightmare. Due to the light, I could clearly see that the spiral stairs were coming to an end. I could see the bottom. I ran for the light, if what you can call my hopping on one leg while dragging the other a run. I tripped and rolled the rest of the way to the bottom. Thankfully, there had only been a dozen steps left to go before I fell.

# 44

# Where Now?

Instead of being back at the hospital, I entered a church where I saw myself serving chili to the homeless. At first, I couldn't remember ever being there, but then in a rush of familiarity, it all came back to me. I had volunteered to serve chili at a church function. I stood behind the table and holding a ladle, I dipped it into the huge pot of hot chili before me. I emptied the contents into a bowl and handed it to the person in front of me. Again, I filled the ladle and emptied it into another bowl. I handed this bowl to an old woman ... the old woman from the hospital.

"This is very nice of you," she had said to me.

"Thank you," I replied. "I volunteer every day the soup kitchen is open."

I realized right then that I had not given any of the glory to God. I had boasted in my own works. I couldn't take it back. I wanted to stop and talk to her, but I couldn't. This was a memory, it had already happened, and I was reliving it exactly as it had happened. I filled another bowl and reached out to hand the chili to the next person in line. I watched as once again the man in line slowly reached into his coat and pulled out a gun. Aiming the gun at me, without hesitation he pulled the trigger and shot me for no apparent reason. "No!" I screamed, but it was too late. The bullet already penetrated me. Once again, I fell, and then I could feel a pain in my torso. I looked down and saw the bullet hole. Blood stained the surrounding area. My mind was in a whirl.

# 45

## The Realistic Truth

At the bottom, I could see that I had only made it to a deep chasm, and there I was still surrounded by rock. Stunned, I wept more than I had all the times before. I was dead. I had to catch my breath, but there was no air to breathe. The panic for air was intense, but I did not pass out, nor did I die. I wasn't breathing. I didn't seem to need oxygen to live down here. I guess there is more to it than just being good to guarantee a place in Heaven. The pastor was right. I had to believe. I never believed or perhaps I kind of believed, but figured I could avoid Hell anyway. Isn't that what everyone believes anyway, at least those who accept that there is a higher being, that by being good we automatically get into Heaven or paradise? If we all believe it, and I ended up here, then won't everyone end up here, too? How do you get to Heaven? No one is perfect.

I was still good, more good than bad.

"Why am I here?" I yelled.

A voice from the darkness, from a far corner of the cave echoed out, "Well, I would say you were here for me, but you're not. I haven't had the desire to ravish a woman since I came to this place. Then again, you do tempt me."

The man that slid out from his hiding place frightened me into a frozen state. He wore a stained t-shirt with a pair of old jeans. The left side of his body appeared as though he had been dipped into a vat of acid. Pus filled blisters covered that part of his face and arm. The right side of his body at first appeared fine, then as he inched closer to me, I could see the same insects on him, eating away at his right arm, as the ones eating away at me. Too frightened to move, I sat still as he placed an arm around my shoulder and continued to seduce me.

"My thirst for blood only nauseates me now, and yet, I can't get the sensation from my mind. Welcome to Hell, love. I'm your worst nightmare."

I unwrapped his arm from around me and tried to inch away. "Who are you?" I asked, though I had an idea that I knew already.

"I am known by many names." The blistered arm fell across me while he held me to the ground with the rest of his weight. I couldn't move. When he continued, I shivered with each answer. "Psychopath, murderer, rapist! Take your pick."

He could see the added terror in my eyes, and I could see the thrill in his eyes, and then the thrill ended. I slid from beneath him and stood the best I could, staring down at him, not knowing what he would do next. I tried to back away, but with one shattered leg and the other broken in several places, my effort for movement was slow at best.

He gathered himself and the thrill was back in his eyes. "I would go on but you seem to understand who I am. Actually, your question should have been: what am I?" He stood up.

I replied, "I know what you are, and I want you to stay away from me." I moved closer to a rock wall and then quickly stepped away when I felt my back begin to burn. Feeling my back, I knew that it now consisted of exposed bone with little flesh left to hide anything. I could feel the insects begin to cover the newly exposed area.

Dragging his left side, the monster moved in on me. I could see a rope wrapped around his hands as if he intended to strangle me. "Now, now, why would I want to do that?" Before I could get away, he grabbed me and tied my arms behind my back. I struggled, but couldn't break or even loosen the bonds. Gloating, he stood back slightly to get a better look. "That's better."

In a shaky voice, I asked, "What do you want with me?" I struggled with the rope a little more and moved away from him.

I finally noticed the fight in his mind. His eyes would look longingly at me one moment and then I could see almost pain and regret. Suddenly he broke down into a mess of tears. Between sobs, he said, "I don't want to hurt you! I cannot help it. This desire will not stop. I remember every victim," he confessed. "I never felt, never knew an emotion before I was cast into this pit of Hell. I am now cursed with feeling every torment I put on every victim. I walk in regret and I cannot separate myself from it. It is bound to me, like a chain around my heart. I have even come across some of my victims here. I cannot bring them comfort. They hate me and I hate me. They fear me and they should, because what I did to them in life, I am doing to them all over again in death. I feel their pain and I cannot stop! I find new victims and I find no satisfaction. I hurt for them. I hurt for you, but I must do this." He paused, but only for a moment or perhaps for longer, it does not matter. "Not only am I able to rape over and over, forced to relive what I did in life, save for also murder—I cannot murder here—I, too, am raped and tormented by the demons at every turn."

Did he want me to feel sorry for him? I did not, nor could I.

Terrified, I shouted, "Let me go!" Though I did not want him close enough to me to actually untie the rope himself.

He seemed to sober up from my outburst, and I immediately regretted opening my mouth. It was as though he was a dual personality, and one of him felt the regret of his actions and the other felt nothing at all.

"Why would I let you go? I never let any of the other women go." He stepped toward me and I, countering his move, stepped back and fell. On the ground, my attempt to free myself proved even more difficult. Dropping down, he put the right side of his face against mine. Tauntingly, he whispered in my ear, "How's this, I'll let you go if you can untie that knot." He already knew that I couldn't. He had been watching as I struggled. He lifted his face from mine and jeeringly laughed at me. My effort with the knot was in vain. I cried into my chest. "It's your own fault anyway. You let me trap you. Deep down you probably wanted this."

I shook violently and shouted, "I do not! Never! Never!" I lunged at him the best I could with the full weight of my body, what was left of it and fell forward.

"I'm sorry," he said and then as if he had not even been bothered by my plea, he teased me even more. "You know the best thing about Hell is that when I'm through with you, I can do it all over again, because you never die."

I closed my eyes, willing him to just disappear. It had worked for some of the creatures before, and I begged that it would happen again. I opened my eyes and saw him still there. A tear was being wiped away from his eye.

"Why me?" I asked. "I didn't do anything to you. I don't belong here!"

His eyes softened for a fraction of a moment and then became hard, "Because you are here, you deserve anything that I choose to do to you." He moved closer to me so that I could feel the puss oozing from his sores. "I took women, like yourself," he brushed my hair out of my face, "and freed them from the bonds of holiness, purity, righteousness, and gave them lust and pain and then death." He paused as if reminiscing in a past event, then the past event became painful for him. He turned his attention back to me. "You know, you're very pretty." He tried to kiss me, but I moved my head to prevent the nauseating union. "You don't have to fight me. Down here you're already tainted, not pure, not worthy of me. I won't harm you. There's nothing to harm."

Again, he reminisced but this time he burst into tears. After what could be considered a minute of crying, since time is no longer a variable it could have been a decade or a second, he stopped. Wiping his face dry, he looked at me with a fierceness that scared me to shake. "I think I'll strangle you and cut out your heart with my small pocket knife. I used to do that to all of my victims."

I squirmed, as he pulled out a small knife, rusted with blood, and placed it at my throat. In a sawing motion, he moved the knife back and forth across my throat slicing through the skin. I screamed. A new source of blood poured from the wound on my neck. The loud outburst startled him and he looked down at my stomach. "Look, you already have a wound." He took the knife and pointed at the bullet hole. "Is the bullet still in there? Shall I dig it out for you?" He commenced to poke the knife into the hole in my torso. Again, I let out a scream of terror and pain. "Calm down! You're too excitable." The man tossed the knife to the side and with his blistered hand stroked my hair, which fell out with each touch.

In a softer tone, he said, "Who I was, what I was among the living is not what I am here among the dead. Here, I'm just like you. None of our sins separates us from the others. We are all the same: heathens, sinners, unrighteous, unholy, murderers, rapists, blasphemers, adulterers, idolaters, thieves, apart from all that is good."

I did not even notice he had disappeared. For a long while, I sat, tied, on the ground that came alive with insects. He was going to come back. I knew he would. I was left there to wait for him.

Numbness came over me. The pain was still there, the fear was still there, but hope was absolutely gone. There wasn't even a grain of hope left. I couldn't muster up a fleck. A low groan echoed off the walls. "What was that? Who's there? Won't you speak comfort to me? Oh, go away! Go away! I don't want to hear any more. I don't want to feel any more." I wanted to die all over again. I wanted to cease my existence in death. I wanted my eternal suffering to end even if it meant that I no longer was. I stood and turned to face the stairs. In desperation, I went for them. I was able to move backward, but before I reached them, the rocks closed up and the stairs disappeared. I crumbled to the ground next to the wall, when the pain continued to climb, I moved and realized that the rope had been burned off.

I was trapped. I had finally made it to my own cavern. I knew there were others walking past my cavern who could see my pathetic state, and though I could not see them, I knew they suffered as I did.

# 46

## Welcome to Hell

There are those that spew from their mouths that 'Hell does not exist,' that 'God would not be a loving God if He sent His people there.' Well, He doesn't. We, who are here, are not God's people. We rejected Him and the truth, the simple truth that He loves us, that He loved us so much that He already paid the price so that we would not have to suffer pain in death. Instead, we cannot fathom that kind of love, we reject it, and never receive it.

We believed the lies that 'Hell wasn't real,' but those were words spoken in fear of the truth, because, if Hell were real, then we would have to do something to prevent from going there. There would be consequences to our actions, to our deeds, that are dealt by a higher power than ourselves. It was so simple, just to love and believe in a Christ that loved and died for us. But with all the lies and fears, we ignored the truth. How simple it would have been, and yet, we chose to believe the lie. Still, it was not God who put us here, but we put ourselves here.

We were given free will to choose and in our selfishness we chose to ignore Him. No amount of sin can ever enter Heaven. That is why God sent His son to die for us. Just by accepting that Christ died, to pay the debt for our sins, He would have cleansed our spirit, that we could enter Heaven and avoid this eternal torment.

There is Good, and there is Evil. There is a God, and there is Satan. There is Heaven, and there is Hell! I am here to tell you that Hell does exist! Those that believe that this place does not exist are fighting the fact that they will one day find themselves here. You can fight all you want, but you'll still find yourself being enveloped in the flame. Fear won't keep you out. There is no end to existence. People will read this and be angry with me, but I don't care. They have to know the truth.

Getting angry with me for opening your eyes to reality will not make this place go away. You ask: 'Will a God of love really torture people throughout eternity? Will the fire of Hell ever burn the wickedness out of sinners?' The fires of Hell are not meant to burn wickedness out. They are the consequence of our belief that we could save ourselves. God does not torture people. When we die, without the knowledge of Christ in our hearts, we are not pure enough to enter Heaven. We are forgotten. God no longer knows us. Our spirit is sent to Hell to face judgment and justice. We are all sinners apart from God, but with the gift of Jesus Christ, who died for our sins, His sacrifice makes it possible for us to enter Heaven. All we have to do is believe. Please, don't end up like me, or do, I don't care. That choice is yours. I've laid before you the truth; it is up to you what you do with it.

"Oh, God, this is Hell! How?"

This place is not a dream. I'm not in a coma. I'm not in the caves of some volcano. I'm not at the edge of the universe. I am in Hell. I am not dreaming, and I am not getting out of this. God cannot hear my pleas, for I am forever separated from Him. This is not some delusion or hallucination. This is Hell. I have been traveling down the corridors of Hell, seeing death at every corner. I am dead. I am death. This is all real. I chose this.

Do you hear me? Do you understand me? I chose this. We have a choice. I had a choice and this … this is what I chose!

You stubborn, foolish people! You have a choice! No one is twisting your arm. No one is forcing you. No one twisted my arm, but even if they had, I still would not have chosen God in my heart. It is more than words—it is heart. I chose chains and bondage. I chose to represent myself before the perfect Judge, and that is why I was found guilty.

I am guilty, and this place is real. The pain is real. The hurt is real. The darkness and evil are real. I am in Hell, not figuratively, but in reality. The flames are real. The monsters are real.

I tried my best to focus on another place, even the hospital. My mind willed and wished, I was even able to envision another place, and yet, I could not get out of there like I had before. Had I really left Hell the other times? I focused on the hospital, the hospital bed, until I burst the veins in my brain. I could not escape. I focused on the white room. I remained in Hell.

The shadow monsters entered the cavern and transformed into tangible, dark creatures. They stood up on their hind legs and came at me, grabbing at my breast, my ear, my thigh, and my arm. The death grip they had on these parts of my body championed everything imaginable on earth. The fierceness, the necessity, the derision I could feel in their claws and teeth as they twisted and ripped those body parts from all connection to me was more than intense than the pain I felt from their sudden and quite conscious removal. I wailed and crumbled over in excruciation. With well over one hundred miles per hour strength, they hurled the pieces of my torn body back at me, impaling me with my own breast, ear, thigh muscle and arm. I was now looking just like the other creatures I had seen down here.

The action caused my stomach to churn and my esophagus to jump into action. I don't know how but I was beginning to vomit. Suddenly part of my intestines were projected onto the floor. I wanted it to be over, but I knew ... I knew this would go on forever.

"Why?" I shouted. "Wasn't I good enough for you? Damn Hollywood!" Again they get it all wrong! We tried so desperately to ignore the bad, pretend that evil didn't exist, that Hell was only for the harden criminals—those that were caught and thrown in prison—that even in death we would have a chance to escape Hell—that by doing one really good thing we would get our wings and be part of the Heavenly Choir. We forgot that if there is a Heaven, there is a Hell. If there is good, there is evil. There is a God and there is a Satan. If Hollywood had done the true story, either the movie would have been super short: well, the evil person died and went to Hell, the end. Or, the movie would have taken the ratings to new standards.

"I should have been better! I could have been better, if I really tried. I just didn't try hard enough," I said shamefully. "I gave everything, but I should have given more. I wanted to; many times I wanted to give more ... more money, more time, more effort. I wasn't perfect. I needed to be perfect. You, God, deserve perfect. I deserve this. I was a horrible person. I lied occasionally, and had unfaithful thoughts – though, I never acted on them; I even rebuked myself. I never forgave that boss for making my life miserable in the office. I should have forgiven her. I didn't want to forgive her. She didn't deserve my mercy. She was the spawn of Satan, not me. She was the one off her rocker, not me. She was the one who was nice one moment and stabbing you in the back the next. She never appreciated me, at least, never in action. In words, she could kiss your feet, praise you till you were sick to your stomach, but in actions, she treated you like an idiot, belittling you till you had no self-confidence in your work and, at times, in yourself. I still don't want to forgive her. She deserves no mercy.

I am only sharing with you pieces of what I am facing here. You cannot imagine … you cannot fathom the shame, the rage, the fear … I am so afraid … at times, I literally am afraid for my life, which is comical to you, but I have seen people die over and over and over again here. Those that committed suicide, kill themselves over and over and over, no pause between kills, no break, but an endless, continual suicide. They cry and weep, screaming to stop, but are forced to continue the action for eternity. Fathom that!

There was an ore and gem mine. Men and women were digging away at the walls which glistened with diamonds, gold, other precious stones and minerals, however once the silver, gold or gem was removed from the wall it immediately revealed its true composition—worthless rock. They were all chained together with heavy chains binding their necks, wrists and ankles. These people had worshiped money in their previous existence. Not all of them had been wealthy—one doesn't have to be wealthy to have a fixation on money. But now, because of their greed, because of their desire, they are here forced to dig and fill the chests that were attached to the already weighted chains. Charles Dickens was correct when he wrote "I now wear the chains I forged in life." The chains that they forged in life they were now forced to wear in death. The only problem with Dickens' story is that in reality Marley was not allowed to leave

Hell once he got here. He would have never been able to warn Scrooge – another one of society's deceptions.

Satan would never allow his captives to go free to help save those still alive from choosing God over him. How stupid do you have to be to believe that? Evil is evil—not very bad with a tendency to do good. Any 'good' that is done not of God is pure deception, counterfeit.

You see the truth is when you die your spirit, your essence, goes to either one of two places: Heaven or Hell. Depending on one choice while you are alive decides where you will spend eternity. If you choose not to believe, to take all this as just another story, you will eventually face the truth whether you want to or not. And once you are in Heaven or Hell, you do not leave—you don't become a demon or an angel. Demons and angels are of a totally different classification, of a different species.

So, with that being said, for those of you who have or know of those who have seen a ghost—a familiar spirit, for those who have communicated with that ghost or familiar spirit—do you now realize that it was not your dead grandmother, your dearly departed uncle, a previous living resident of the house? Do you realize that it was a deception by a demonic being, which is forced to walk the earth? A demonic being that once walked and frolicked in Heaven, which chose to follow Satan and is now punished by never standing in God's presence again! These demons—once angels who were the spirits of Love, spirits of life, spirits of Hope, spirits of Joy, spirits of Peace, spirits of Truth, spirits of Righteousness, spirits of Health—are now the spirits of fear, spirits of hate, spirits of death, spirits of abandonment, spirits of lies, spirits of infirmity. Sure these demons may tell facts, but at what cost do you listen to them? Continue to listen and you will find out the cost.

"I hate You!" I shouted to God. "I wasted my life on You! I wasted my life working so hard to please You, doing good works. I never killed more than a cockroach. I only told white lies. I never coveted my neighbors' property. I never had an affair. I never worshiped other gods. I went to church on Sundays. I never stole." I picked up a skull from the ground and slammed it into the wall and watched it shatter; a scream came from the pieces, distracting my thoughts for only a moment. "I hate You! You abandoned me! What did You want from me? To choose You? Weren't the good works enough? To forgive? Why? I wasn't forgiven! You didn't forgive me or I wouldn't be down here! I loathe You! You don't want to look at me? Well, I don't want to look at You!" I spun around in frustration and pulled at my arm in agony, peeling off my flesh, hoping that stripping off the flesh I could be made clean. "I'm sorry! I didn't mean it!" I shouted to the ceiling of the tunnel. I forgive. I choose You. Please, help me! Take me out of here! I'm sorry! Are You deaf? I said I choose You, now take me out of here!" I ordered. "I hate You! I hate You! I wish You never existed! Then I wouldn't be here!" The absurdity! If God, the creator of all, had never existed, then I wouldn't exist. To exist. What is it to not exist? My mind cannot wrap around the question.

Suddenly, I felt the ground shake. My screams had caused an echo and a vibration in the cavern. Trying to balance, the ground cracked directly beneath my feet and a burst of fire leapt out consuming me. In one last plea, I faced Heaven and let out a deafening scream.

When I opened my eyes, there was complete darkness. I wondered if someone had turned off the lights. It was so dark. I was standing and soon realized that the ground beneath me was rocky and sandy. After shouting, pleading for someone to turn on the lights, I realized that I was completely alone. Shock and fear settled on me. I hated being alone, I never wanted to be left alone again, which startled me since I had been okay with being left alone before. This was different. There was an absence and abandonment feeling in the atmosphere, as though I would never see anyone again, as though I was now ultimately alone.

I hated those who had left me here. I began to think of rather evil ways to get back at them for abandoning me here. I would get even. I would show them. And yet, as I have said, I knew deep down ... deep down I knew that I would never see anyone again, that I was completely alone.

How long could I last here? Where is here? The air felt stagnant, old; it choked to breathe it in. Was I actually breathing? I had to be breathing. If I was not breathing, I would be dead. I hurt all over, so I must not be dead. The pain ... how to describe the pain ... my insides felt like they were being shredded by broken glass. My bones felt as though they were all broken. My skin felt as though someone was pulling every last hair out of me at the same time. My head felt as though all the blood vessels had exploded.

I began to shout in fear, screaming at the top of my lungs, pleading and begging for anyone to hear me. I would even settle for an animal or a bug, but not even that came to me.

Where am I? Who am I? These questions plagued me.

A dim orangey glow brightened the area enough for me to see that I was in a cave. My eyes fell to an entrance or an exit. When I stepped over to it, I could see the steps which had been cut from solid rock using bare hands.

Someone somewhere shouted, "You have been found guilty! You are guilty!"

These words echoed along with the screams of billions of voices in pain.

It wasn't long when I remembered where I was. Looking down, I placed my foot on the first step and began my agonizing

204

descent. Perhaps this time, I would find the way out.
Welcome to Hell.